Henry VIII

By William Shakespeare

A Digireads.com Book
Digireads.com Publishing

Henry VIII
By William Shakespeare
ISBN: 1-4209-3217-9

This edition copyright © 2009

Please visit *www.digireads.com*

DRAMATIS PERSONAE

KING HENRY THE EIGHTH
CARDINAL WOLSEY
CARDINAL CAMPEIUS
CAPUCIUS, *Ambassador from the Emperor Charles V*
CRANMER, *Archbishop of Canterbury*
DUKE OF NORFOLK
DUKE OF BUCKINGHAM
DUKE OF SUFFOLK
EARL OF SURREY
Lord Chamberlain
Lord Chancellor
GARDINER, *Bishop of Winchester*
Bishop of Lincoln
LORD ABERGAVENNY
LORD SANDYS
SIR HENRY GUILDFORD
SIR THOMAS LOVELL
SIR ANTHONY DENNY
SIR NICHOLAS VAUX
Secretaries to Wolsey
CROMWELL, *servant to Wolsey*
GRIFFITH, *gentleman-usher to Queen Katherine*
Three Gentlemen
DOCTOR BUTTS, *physician to the King*
Garter King-at-Arms
Surveyor to the Duke of Buckingham
BRANDON, *and a Sergeant-at-Arms*
Door-keeper of the Council-chamber
Porter, and his Man
Page to Gardiner
A Crier
QUEEN KATHERINE, *wife to King Henry, afterwards divorced*
ANNE BULLEN, *her Maid of Honour, afterwards Queen*
An old Lady, friend to Anne Bullen
PATIENCE, *woman to Queen Katherine*
Lord Mayor, Alderman, Lords and Ladies in the Dumb Shows; Women attending upon the Queen; Scribes, Officers, Guards, and other Attendants, and Spirits.

THE SCENE: LONDON; WESTMINSTER; KIMBOLTON

THE PROLOGUE

I come no more to make you laugh: things now
That bear a weighty and a serious brow,
Sad, high, and working, full of state and woe,
Such noble scenes as draw the eye to flow,
We now present. Those that can pity, here
May, if they think it well, let fall a tear;
The subject will deserve it. Such as give
Their money out of hope they may believe,
May here find truth too. Those that come to see
Only a show or two, and so agree
The play may pass, if they be still and willing,
I'll undertake may see away their shilling
Richly in two short hours. Only they
That come to hear a merry bawdy play,
A noise of targets, or to see a fellow
In a long motley coat guarded with yellow,
Will be deceiv'd; for, gentle hearers, know,
To rank our chosen truth with such a show
As fool and fight is, beside forfeiting
Our own brains, and the opinion that we bring
To make that only true we now intend,
Will leave us never an understanding friend.
Therefore, for goodness' sake, and as you are known
The first and happiest hearers of the town,
Be sad, as we would make ye; think ye see
The very persons of our noble story
As they were living; think you see them great,
And follow'd with the general throng and sweat
Of thousand friends; then, in a moment, see
How soon this mightiness meets misery;
And if you can be merry then, I'll say
A man may weep upon his wedding-day.

ACT I.

SCENE I. *London. The palace.*

[*Enter the DUKE OF NORFOLK at one door; at the other, the DUKE OF BUCKINGHAM and the LORD ABERGAVENNY.*]

BUCKINGHAM. Good morrow, and well met. How have ye done
　　Since last we saw in France?

NORFOLK. I thank your Grace,
　　Healthful; and ever since a fresh admirer
　　Of what I saw there.

BUCKINGHAM. An untimely ague
　　Stay'd me a prisoner in my chamber when
　　Those suns of glory, those two lights of men,
　　Met in the vale of Andren.

NORFOLK. 'Twixt Guynes and Arde—
　　I was then present, saw them salute on horseback;
　　Beheld them, when they lighted, how they clung
　　In their embracement, as they grew together;
　　Which had they, what four thron'd ones could have weigh'd
　　Such a compounded one?

BUCKINGHAM. All the whole time
　　I was my chamber's prisoner.

NORFOLK. Then you lost
　　The view of earthly glory. Men might say,
　　Till this time pomp was single, but now married
　　To one above itself. Each following day
　　Became the next day's master, till the last
　　Made former wonders its. To-day the French,
　　All clinquant, all in gold, like heathen gods,
　　Shone down the English; and, to-morrow, they
　　Made Britain India: every man that stood
　　Show'd like a mine. Their dwarfish pages were
　　As cherubins, all gilt; the madams too,
　　Not us'd to toil, did almost sweat to bear
　　The pride upon them, that their very labour
　　Was to them as a painting. Now this masque
　　Was cried incomparable; and the ensuing night
　　Made it a fool and beggar. The two kings,
　　Equal in lustre, were now best, now worst,
　　As presence did present them; him in eye,

Still him in praise; and, being present both,
'Twas said they saw but one; and no discerner
Durst wag his tongue in censure. When these suns—
For so they phrase 'em—by their heralds challeng'd
The noble spirits to arms, they did perform
Beyond thought's compass, that former fabulous story,
Being now seen possible enough, got credit,
That Bevis was believ'd.

BUCKINGHAM. O, you go far!

NORFOLK. As I belong to worship and affect
In honour honesty, the tract of ev'rything
Would by a good discourser lose some life,
Which action's self was tongue to. All was royal;
To the disposing of it nought rebell'd,
Order gave each thing view; the office did
Distinctly his full function.

BUCKINGHAM. Who did guide,
I mean, who set the body and the limbs
Of this great sport together, as you guess?

NORFOLK. One, certes, that promises no element
In such a business.

BUCKINGHAM. I pray you, who, my lord?

NORFOLK. All this was ord'red by the good discretion
Of the right reverend Cardinal of York.

BUCKINGHAM. The devil speed him! no man's pie is freed
From his ambitious finger. What had he
To do in these fierce vanities? I wonder
That such a keech can with his very bulk
Take up the rays o' th' beneficial sun,
And keep it from the earth.

NORFOLK. Surely, sir,
There's in him stuff that puts him to these ends;
For, being not propp'd by ancestry, whose grace
Chalks successors their way, nor call'd upon
For high feats done to the crown; neither allied
To eminent assistants; but, spider-like,
Out of his self-drawing web, he gives us note,
The force of his own merit makes his way;
A gift that heaven gives for him, which buys
A place next to the King.

ABERGAVENNY. I cannot tell
    What heaven hath given him,—let some graver eye
    Pierce into that; but I can see his pride
    Peep through each part of him. Whence has he that?
    If not from hell, the devil is a niggard,
    Or has given all before, and he begins
    A new hell in himself.

BUCKINGHAM. Why the devil,
    Upon this French going out, took he upon him,
    Without the privity o' the King, to appoint
    Who should attend on him? He makes up the file
    Of all the gentry; for the most part such
    To whom as great a charge as little honour
    He meant to lay upon; and his own letter,
    The honourable board of council out,
    Must fetch him in he papers.

ABERGAVENNY. I do know
    Kinsmen of mine, three at the least, that have
    By this so sicken'd their estates, that never
    They shall abound as formerly.

BUCKINGHAM. O, many
    Have broke their backs with laying manors on 'em
    For this great journey. What did this vanity
    But minister communication of
    A most poor issue?

NORFOLK. Grievingly I think
    The peace between the French and us not values
    The cost that did conclude it.

BUCKINGHAM. Every man,
    After the hideous storm that follow'd, was
    A thing inspir'd; and, not consulting, broke
    Into a general prophecy, that this tempest,
    Dashing the garment of this peace, aboded
    The sudden breach on't.

NORFOLK. Which is budded out;
    For France hath flaw'd the league, and hath attach'd
    Our merchants' goods at Bordeaux.

ABERGAVENNY. Is it therefore
    The ambassador is silenc'd?

NORFOLK. Marry, is't.

ABERGAVENNY. A proper title of a peace, and purchas'd
  At a superfluous rate!

BUCKINGHAM. Why, all this business
  Our reverend Cardinal carried.

NORFOLK. Like it your Grace,
  The state takes notice of the private difference
  Betwixt you and the Cardinal. I advise you—
  And take it from a heart that wishes towards you
  Honour and plenteous safety—that you read
  The Cardinal's malice and his potency
  Together, to consider further that
  What his high hatred would effect wants not
  A minister in his power. You know his nature,
  That he's revengeful, and I know his sword
  Hath a sharp edge; it's long, and, 't may be said,
  It reaches far, and where 'twill not extend,
  Thither he darts it. Bosom up my counsel,
  You'll find it wholesome. Lo, where comes that rock
  That I advise your shunning.

  [*Enter CARDINAL WOLSEY, the purse borne before him, certain of the Guard,
    and two Secretaries, with papers. The Cardinal in his passage fixeth his eye
    on Buckingham, and Buckingham on him, both full of disdain.*]

WOLSEY. The Duke of Buckingham's surveyor, ha?
  Where's his examination?

SECRETARY. Here, so please you.

WOLSEY. Is he in person ready?

SECRETARY. Ay, please your Grace.

WOLSEY. Well, we shall then know more; and Buckingham
  Shall lessen this big look.

  [*Exeunt Wolsey and his Train.*]

BUCKINGHAM. This butcher's cur is venom-mouth'd, and I
  Have not the power to muzzle him; therefore best
  Not wake him in his slumber. A beggar's book
  Outworths a noble's blood.

NORFOLK. What, are you chaf'd?
  Ask God for temp'rance; that's the appliance only
  Which your disease requires.

BUCKINGHAM. I read in 's looks
  Matter against me, and his eye revil'd
  Me as his abject object. At this instant
  He bores me with some trick. He's gone to the King;
  I'll follow, and outstare him.

NORFOLK. Stay, my lord,
  And let your reason with your choler question
  What 'tis you go about. To climb steep hills
  Requires slow pace at first. Anger is like
  A full hot horse, who being allow'd his way,
  Self-mettle tires him. Not a man in England
  Can advise me like you; be to yourself
  As you would to your friend.

BUCKINGHAM. I'll to the King,
  And from a mouth of honour quite cry down
  This Ipswich fellow's insolence, or proclaim
  There's difference in no persons.

NORFOLK. Be advis'd;
  Heat not a furnace for your foe so hot
  That it do singe yourself. We may outrun,
  By violent swiftness, that which we run at,
  And lose by over-running. Know you not,
  The fire that mounts the liquor till 't run o'er,
  In seeming to augment it wastes it? Be advis'd.
  I say again, there is no English soul
  More stronger to direct you than yourself,
  If with the sap of reason you would quench,
  Or but allay, the fire of passion.

BUCKINGHAM. Sir,
  I am thankful to you; and I'll go along
  By your prescription; but this top-proud fellow,
  Whom from the flow of gall I name not, but
  From sincere motions, by intelligence,
  And proofs as clear as founts in July when
  We see each grain of gravel, I do know
  To be corrupt and treasonous.

NORFOLK. Say not "treasonous."

BUCKINGHAM. To the King I'll say't, and make my vouch as strong
    As shore of rock. Attend. This holy fox,
    Or wolf, or both,—for he is equal ravenous
    As he is subtle, and as prone to mischief
    As able to perform't; his mind and place
    Infecting one another, yea, reciprocally—
    Only to show his pomp as well in France
    As here at home, suggests the King our master
    To this last costly treaty, the interview,
    That swallowed so much treasure, and like a glass
    Did break i' the rinsing.

NORFOLK. Faith, and so it did.

BUCKINGHAM. Pray, give me favour, sir. This cunning Cardinal
    The articles o' the combination drew
    As himself pleas'd; and they were ratified
    As he cried "Thus let be," to as much end
    As give a crutch to the dead. But our count-cardinal
    Has done this, and 'tis well; for worthy Wolsey,
    Who cannot err, he did it. Now this follows,
    Which, as I take it, is a kind of puppy
    To the old dam, treason: Charles the Emperor,
    Under pretence to see the Queen his aunt,—
    For 'twas indeed his colour, but he came
    To whisper Wolsey,—here makes visitation.
    His fears were, that the interview betwixt
    England and France might, through their amity,
    Breed him some prejudice; for from this league
    Peep'd harms that menac'd him. He privily
    Deals with our Cardinal; and, as I trow,—
    Which I do well, for I am sure the Emperor
    Paid ere he promis'd; whereby his suit was granted
    Ere it was ask'd—but when the way was made,
    And pav'd with gold, the Emperor thus desir'd,
    That he would please to alter the King's course,
    And break the foresaid peace. Let the King know,
    As soon he shall by me, that thus the Cardinal
    Does buy and sell his honour as he pleases
    And for his own advantage.

NORFOLK. I am sorry
    To hear this of him; and could wish he were
    Something mistaken in't.

BUCKINGHAM. No, not a syllable:
    I do pronounce him in that very shape
    He shall appear in proof.

[*Enter BRANDON, a Sergeant-at-Arms before him, and two or three of the Guard.*]

BRANDON. Your office, sergeant; execute it.

SERGEANT. Sir,
    My lord the Duke of Buckingham, and Earl
    Of Hereford, Stafford, and Northampton, I
    Arrest thee of high treason, in the name
    Of our most sovereign king.

BUCKINGHAM. Lo, you, my lord,
    The net has fall'n upon me! I shall perish
    Under device and practice.

BRANDON. I am sorry
    To see you ta'en from liberty, to look on
    The business present. 'Tis his Highness' pleasure
    You shall to the Tower.

BUCKINGHAM. It will help nothing
    To plead mine innocence; for that dye is on me
    Which makes my whit'st part black. The will of Heaven
    Be done in this and all things! I obey.
    O my Lord Abergavenny, fare you well!

BRANDON. Nay, he must bear you company.
    [*To Abergavenny.*] The King
    Is pleas'd you shall to the Tower, till you know
    How he determines further.

ABERGAVENNY. As the Duke said,
    The will of Heaven be done, and the King's pleasure
    By me obey'd!

BRANDON. Here is warrant from
    The King to attach Lord Montacute, and the bodies
    Of the Duke's confessor, John de la Car,
    One Gilbert Peck, his chancellor,—

BUCKINGHAM. So, so;
    These are the limbs o' the plot. No more, I hope?

BRANDON. A monk o' the Chartreux.

BUCKINGHAM. O, Nicholas Hopkins?

BRANDON. He.

BUCKINGHAM. My surveyor is false; the o'er-great Cardinal
    Hath show'd him gold; my life is spann'd already.
    I am the shadow of poor Buckingham,
    Whose figure even this instant cloud puts on,
    By dark'ning my clear sun. My lord, farewell.

[*Exeunt.*]

SCENE II. *London. The Council Chamber.*

[*Cornets. Enter KING HENRY, leaning on the CARDINAL'S shoulder, the
Nobles, and SIR THOMAS LOVELL with Others. The Cardinal places
himself under the King's feet on his right side.*]

KING. My life itself, and the best heart of it,
    Thanks you for this great care. I stood i' the level
    Of a full-charg'd confederacy, and give thanks
    To you that chok'd it. Let be call'd before us
    That gentleman of Buckingham's; in person
    I'll hear his confessions justify;
    And point by point the treasons of his master
    He shall again relate.

[*A noise within, crying "Room for the Queen!" Enter the QUEEN, ushered by
the DUKES OF NORFOLK, and SUFFOLK; she kneels. The King riseth
from his state, takes her up, kisses and placeth her by him.*]

QUEEN KATHERINE. Nay, we must longer kneel; I am a suitor.

KING. Arise, and take place by us. Half your suit
    Never name to us, you have half our power;
    The other moiety, ere you ask, is given.
    Repeat your will and take it.

QUEEN KATHERINE. Thank your Majesty.
    That you would love yourself, and in that love
    Not unconsidered leave your honour, nor
    The dignity of your office, is the point
    Of my petition.

KING. Lady mine, proceed.

QUEEN KATHERINE. I am solicited, not by a few,
    And those of true condition, that your subjects
    Are in great grievance. There have been commissions
    Sent down among 'em, which hath flaw'd the heart
    Of all their loyalties; wherein, although,

My good Lord Cardinal, they vent reproaches
Most bitterly on you, as putter on
Of these exactions, yet the King our master—
Whose honour Heaven shield from soil!—even he escapes not
Language unmannerly, yea, such which breaks
The sides of loyalty, and almost appears
In loud rebellion.

NORFOLK. Not "almost appears,"
It doth appear; for, upon these taxations,
The clothiers all, not able to maintain
The many to them longing, have put off
The spinsters, carders, fullers, weavers, who,
Unfit for other life, compell'd by hunger
And lack of other means, in desperate manner
Daring the event to the teeth, are all in uproar,
And danger serves among them.

KING. Taxation!
Wherein? and what taxation? My Lord Cardinal,
You that are blam'd for it alike with us,
Know you of this taxation?

WOLSEY. Please you, sir,
I know but of a single part, in aught
Pertains to the state, and front but in that file
Where others tell steps with me.

QUEEN KATHERINE. No, my lord?
You know no more than others? But you frame
Things that are known alike, which are not wholesome
To those which would not know them, and yet must
Perforce be their acquaintance. These exactions,
Whereof my sovereign would have note, they are
Most pestilent to the hearing; and, to bear 'em,
The back is sacrifice to the load. They say
They are devis'd by you; or else you suffer
Too hard an exclamation.

KING. Still exaction!
The nature of it? In what kind, let's know,
Is this exaction?

QUEEN KATHERINE. I am much too venturous
In tempting of your patience; but am bold'ned
Under your promis'd pardon. The subjects' grief
Comes through commissions, which compels from each
The sixth part of his substance, to be levied

Without delay; and the pretence for this
Is nam'd, your wars in France. This makes bold mouths;
Tongues spit their duties out, and cold hearts freeze
Allegiance in them; their curses now
Live where their prayers did; and it's come to pass
This tractable obedience is a slave
To each incensed will. I would your Highness
Would give it quick consideration, for
There is no primer business.

KING. By my life,
   This is against our pleasure.

WOLSEY. And for me,
   I have no further gone in this than by
   A single voice; and that not pass'd me but
   By learned approbation of the judges. If I am
   Traduc'd by ignorant tongues, which neither know
   My faculties nor person, yet will be
   The chronicles of my doing, let me say
   'Tis but the fate of place, and the rough brake
   That virtue must go through. We must not stint
   Our necessary actions, in the fear
   To cope malicious censurers; which ever,
   As ravenous fishes, do a vessel follow
   That is new-trimm'd, but benefit no further
   Than vainly longing. What we oft do best,
   By sick interpreters, once weak ones, is
   Not ours, or not allow'd; what worst, as oft,
   Hitting a grosser quality, is cried up
   For our best act. If we shall stand still,
   In fear our motion will be mock'd or carp'd at,
   We should take root here where we sit, or sit
   State-statues only.

KING. Things done well,
   And with a care, exempt themselves from fear;
   Things done without example, in their issue
   Are to be fear'd. Have you a precedent
   Of this commission? I believe, not any.
   We must not rend our subjects from our laws,
   And stick them in our will. Sixth part of each?
   A trembling contribution! Why, we take
   From every tree lop, bark, and part o' the timber;
   And, though we leave it with a root, thus hack'd,
   The air will drink the sap. To every county
   Where this is question'd send our letters, with
   Free pardon to each man that has denied

The force of this commission. Pray, look to't;
I put it to your care.

WOLSEY. [*Aside to the Secretary*] A word with you.
Let there be letters writ to every shire,
Of the King's grace and pardon. The grieved commons
Hardly conceive of me; let it be nois'd
That through our intercession this revokement
And pardon comes. I shall anon advise you
Further in the proceeding.

[*Exit Secretary.*]

[*Enter Surveyor.*]

QUEEN KATHERINE. I am sorry that the Duke of Buckingham
Is run in your displeasure.

KING. It grieves many.
The gentleman is learn'd, and a most rare speaker;
To nature none more bound; his training such
That he may furnish and instruct great teachers,
And never seek for aid out of himself. Yet see,
When these so noble benefits shall prove
Not well dispos'd, the mind growing once corrupt,
They turn to vicious forms, ten times more ugly
Than ever they were fair. This man so complete,
Who was enroll'd 'mongst wonders, and when we,
Almost with ravish'd list'ning, could not find
His hour of speech a minute; he, my lady,
Hath into monstrous habits put the graces
That once were his, and is become as black
As if besmear'd in hell. Sit by us; you shall hear—
This was his gentleman in trust—of him
Things to strike honour sad. Bid him recount
The fore-recited practices, whereof
We cannot feel too little, hear too much.

WOLSEY. Stand forth, and with bold spirit relate what you,
Most like a careful subject, have collected
Out of the Duke of Buckingham.

KING. Speak freely.

SURVEYOR. First, it was usual with him, every day
It would infect his speech, that if the King
Should without issue die, he'll carry it so
To make the sceptre his. These very words

I've heard him utter to his son-in-law,
Lord Abergavenny; to whom by oath he menac'd
Revenge upon the Cardinal.

WOLSEY. Please your Highness, note
This dangerous conception in this point.
Not friended by his wish, to your high person
His will is most malignant; and it stretches
Beyond you, to your friends.

QUEEN KATHERINE. My learn'd Lord Cardinal,
Deliver all with charity.

KING. Speak on.
How grounded he his title to the crown?
Upon our fail? To this point hast thou heard him
At any time speak aught?

SURVEYOR. He was brought to this
By a vain prophecy of Nicholas Henton.

KING. What was that Henton?

SURVEYOR. Sir, a Chartreux friar,
His confessor; who fed him every minute
With words of sovereignty.

KING. How know'st thou this?

SURVEYOR. Not long before your Highness sped to France,
The Duke being at the Rose, within the parish
Saint Lawrence Poultney, did of me demand
What was the speech among the Londoners
Concerning the French journey. I replied,
Men fear the French would prove perfidious,
To the King's danger. Presently the Duke
Said, 'twas the fear, indeed; and that he doubted
'Twould prove the verity of certain words
Spoke by a holy monk, "that oft," says he,
"Hath sent to me, wishing me to permit
John de la Car, my chaplain, a choice hour
To hear from him a matter of some moment;
Whom after under the confession's seal
He solemnly had sworn, that what he spoke
My chaplain to no creature living but
To me should utter, with demure confidence
This pausingly ensu'd: 'Neither the King nor's heirs,
Tell you the Duke, shall prosper. Bid him strive

To gain the love o' the commonalty. The Duke
Shall govern England.'"

QUEEN KATHERINE. If I know you well,
You were the Duke's surveyor, and lost your office
On the complaint o' the tenants. Take good heed
You charge not in your spleen a noble person
And spoil your nobler soul; I say, take heed;
Yes, heartily beseech you.

KING. Let him on.
Go forward.

SURVEYOR. On my soul, I'll speak but truth.
I told my lord the Duke, by the devil's illusions
The monk might be deceiv'd; and that 'twas dangerous for him
To ruminate on this so far, until
It forg'd him some design; which, being believ'd,
It was much like to do. He answer'd, "Tush,
It can do me no damage;" adding further
That, had the King in his last sickness fail'd,
The Cardinal's and Sir Thomas Lovell's heads
Should have gone off.

KING. Ha! what, so rank? Ah ha!
There's mischief in this man. Canst thou say further?

SURVEYOR. I can, my liege.

KING. Proceed.

SURVEYOR. Being at Greenwich,
After your Highness had reprov'd the Duke
About Sir William Bulmer,—

KING. I remember
Of such a time; being my sworn servant,
The Duke retain'd him his. But on; what hence?

SURVEYOR. "If," quoth he, "I for this had been committed,"—
As, to the Tower, I thought,—"I would have play'd
The part my father meant to act upon
The usurper Richard; who, being at Salisbury,
Made suit to come in 's presence; which if granted,
As he made semblance of his duty, would
Have put his knife into him."

KING. A giant traitor!

WOLSEY. Now, madam, may his Highness live in freedom,
    And this man out of prison?

QUEEN KATHERINE. God mend all!

KING. There's something more would out of thee; what say'st?

SURVEYOR. After "the Duke his father," with "the knife,"
    He stretch'd him, and, with one hand on his dagger,
    Another spread on 's breast, mounting his eyes,
    He did discharge a horrible oath; whose tenour
    Was, were he evil us'd, he would outgo
    His father by as much as a performance
    Does an irresolute purpose.

KING. There's his period,
    To sheathe his knife in us. He is attach'd.
    Call him to present trial. If he may
    Find mercy in the law, 'tis his; if none,
    Let him not seek 't of us. By day and night,
    He's traitor to th' height.

[Exeunt.]

SCENE III. *London. The palace.*

[Enter the Lord Chamberlain and LORD SANDYS.]

CHAMBERLAIN. Is't possible the spells of France should juggle
    Men into such strange mysteries?

SANDYS. New customs,
    Though they be never so ridiculous,
    Nay, let 'em be unmanly, yet are follow'd.

CHAMBERLAIN. As far as I see, all the good our English
    Have got by the late voyage is but merely
    A fit or two o' the face; but they are shrewd ones;
    For when they hold 'em, you would swear directly
    Their very noses had been counsellors
    To Pepin or Clotharius, they keep state so.

SANDYS. They have all new legs, and lame ones. One would take it,
    That never saw 'em pace before, the spavin
    Or springhalt reign'd among 'em.

CHAMBERLAIN. Death! my lord,
 Their clothes are after such a pagan cut too,
 That, sure, they've worn out Christendom.

[*Enter SIR THOMAS LOVELL.*]

 How now!
 What news, Sir Thomas Lovell?

LOVELL. Faith, my lord,
 I hear of none, but the new proclamation
 That's clapp'd upon the court-gate.

CHAMBERLAIN. What is't for?

LOVELL. The reformation of our travell'd gallants,
 That fill the court with quarrels, talk, and tailors.

CHAMBERLAIN. I'm glad 'tis there. Now I would pray our monsieurs
 To think an English courtier may be wise,
 And never see the Louvre.

LOVELL. They must either,
 For so run the conditions, leave those remnants
 Of fool and feather that they got in France,
 With all their honourable points of ignorance
 Pertaining thereunto, as fights and fireworks,
 Abusing better men than they can be,
 Out of a foreign wisdom, renouncing clean
 The faith they have in tennis and tall stockings,
 Short blist'red breeches, and those types of travel,
 And understand again like honest men,
 Or pack to their old playfellows. There, I take it,
 They may, "cum privilegio," wear away
 The lag end of their lewdness and be laugh'd at.

SANDYS. 'Tis time to give 'em physic, their diseases
 Are grown so catching.

CHAMBERLAIN. What a loss our ladies
 Will have of these trim vanities!

LOVELL. Ay, marry,
 There will be woe indeed, lords; the sly whoresons
 Have got a speeding trick to lay down ladies.
 A French song and a fiddle has no fellow.

SANDYS. The devil fiddle 'em! I am glad they are going,
    For, sure, there's no converting of 'em. Now
    An honest country lord, as I am, beaten
    A long time out of play, may bring his plainsong
    And have an hour of hearing; and, by 'r Lady,
    Held current music too.

CHAMBERLAIN. Well said, Lord Sandys;
    Your colt's tooth is not cast yet.

SANDYS. No, my lord;
    Nor shall not, while I have a stump.

CHAMBERLAIN. Sir Thomas,
    Whither were you a-going?

LOVELL. To the Cardinal's.
    Your lordship is a guest too.

CHAMBERLAIN. O, 'tis true:
    This night he makes a supper, and a great one,
    To many lords and ladies; there will be
    The beauty of this kingdom, I'll assure you.

LOVELL. That churchman bears a bounteous mind indeed,
    A hand as fruitful as the land that feeds us;
    His dews fall everywhere.

CHAMBERLAIN. No doubt he's noble;
    He had a black mouth that said other of him.

SANDYS. He may, my lord; has wherewithal; in him
    Sparing would show a worse sin than ill doctrine.
    Men of his way should be most liberal;
    They are set here for examples.

CHAMBERLAIN. True, they are so;
    But few now give so great ones. My barge stays;
    Your lordship shall along. Come, good Sir Thomas,
    We shall be late else; which I would not be,
    For I was spoke to, with Sir Henry Guildford,
    This night to be comptrollers.

SANDYS. I am your lordship's.

                         [*Exeunt.*]

SCENE IV. *London. The Presence Chamber in York Place.*

[*Hautboys. A small table under a state for the Cardinal, a longer table for the guests. Then enter ANNE BULLEN and divers other Ladies and Gentlemen as guests, at one door; at another door, enter SIR HENRY GUILDFORD.*]

GUILDFORD. Ladies, a general welcome from his Grace
    Salutes ye all; this night he dedicates
    To fair content and you. None here, he hopes,
    In all this noble bevy, has brought with her
    One care abroad. He would have all as merry
    As, first, good company, good wine, good welcome,
    Can make good people.

[*Enter Lord Chamberlain, LORD SANDYS, and SIR THOMAS LOVELL.*]

    O, my lord, you're tardy;
    The very thought of this fair company
    Clapp'd wings to me.

CHAMBERLAIN. You are young, Sir Harry Guildford.

SANDYS. Sir Thomas Lovell, had the Cardinal
    But half my lay thoughts in him, some of these
    Should find a running banquet ere they rested,
    I think would better please 'em. By my life,
    They are a sweet society of fair ones.

LOVELL. O, that your lordship were but now confessor
    To one or two of these!

SANDYS. I would I were;
    They should find easy penance.

LOVELL. Faith, how easy?

SANDYS. As easy as a down-bed would afford it.

CHAMBERLAIN. Sweet ladies, will it please you sit? Sir Harry,
    Place you that side; I'll take the charge of this.
    His Grace is ent'ring. Nay, you must not freeze;
    Two women plac'd together makes cold weather.
    My Lord Sandys, you are one will keep 'em waking;
    Pray, sit between these ladies.

SANDYS. By my faith,
    And thank your lordship. By your leave, sweet ladies.
    If I chance to talk a little wild, forgive me;
    I had it from my father.

ANNE. Was he mad, sir?

SANDYS. O, very mad, exceeding mad; in love too;
    But he would bite none. Just as I do now,
    He would kiss you twenty with a breath.

                    [*Kisses her.*]

CHAMBERLAIN. Well said, my lord.
    So, now you're fairly seated. Gentlemen,
    The penance lies on you, if these fair ladies
    Pass away frowning.

SANDYS. For my little cure,
    Let me alone.

        [*Hautboys. Enter CARDINAL WOLSEY, attended; and takes his state.*]

WOLSEY. You're welcome, my fair guests. That noble lady
    Or gentleman that is not freely merry
    Is not my friend. This, to confirm my welcome;
    And to you all, good health.

                    [*Drinks.*]

SANDYS. Your Grace is noble.
    Let me have such a bowl may hold my thanks,
    And save me so much talking.

WOLSEY. My Lord Sandys,
    I am beholding to you; cheer your neighbours.
    Ladies, you are not merry. Gentlemen,
    Whose fault is this?

SANDYS. The red wine first must rise
    In their fair cheeks, my lord; then we shall have 'em
    Talk us to silence.

ANNE. You are a merry gamester,
    My Lord Sandys.

SANDYS. Yes, if I make my play.
    Here's to your ladyship; and pledge it, madam,
    For 'tis to such a thing,—

ANNE. You cannot show me.

SANDYS. I told your Grace they would talk anon.

               [Drum and trumpet. Chambers discharged.]

WOLSEY. What's that?

CHAMBERLAIN. Look out there, some of ye.

               [Exit a Servant.]

WOLSEY. What warlike voice,
    And to what end, is this? Nay, ladies, fear not;
    By all the laws of war you're privileg'd.

               [Re-enter Servant.]

CHAMBERLAIN. How now! what is't?

SERVANT. A noble troop of strangers,
    For so they seem. They've left their barge and landed,
    And hither make, as great ambassadors
    From foreign princes.

WOLSEY. Good Lord Chamberlain,
    Go, give 'em welcome; you can speak the French tongue;
    And, pray, receive 'em nobly, and conduct 'em
    Into our presence, where this heaven of beauty
    Shall shine at full upon them. Some attend him.

       [Exit Chamberlain, attended. All rise, and tables remov'd.]

You have now a broken banquet; but we'll mend it.
A good digestion to you all; and once more
I shower a welcome on ye. Welcome all!

*[Hautboys. Enter the KING, and Others, as maskers, habited like shepherds,
    usher'd by the Lord Chamberlain. They pass directly before the Cardinal,
    and gracefully salute him.]*

A noble company! What are their pleasures?

CHAMBERLAIN. Because they speak no English, thus they pray'd
    To tell your Grace, that, having heard by fame
    Of this so noble and so fair assembly
    This night to meet here, they could do no less,
    Out of the great respect they bear to beauty,
    But leave their flocks; and, under your fair conduct,
    Crave leave to view these ladies and entreat
    An hour of revels with 'em.

WOLSEY. Say, Lord Chamberlain,
    They have done my poor house grace; for which I pay 'em
    A thousand thanks, and pray 'em take their pleasures.

        [They choose ladies for the dance. The King chooses Anne Bullen.]

KING. The fairest hand I ever touch'd! O beauty,
    Till now I never knew thee!

        [Music. Dance.]

WOLSEY. My lord!

CHAMBERLAIN. Your Grace?

WOLSEY. Pray, tell 'em thus much from me:
    There should be one amongst 'em, by his person,
    More worthy this place than myself; to whom,
    If I but knew him, with my love and duty
    I would surrender it.

CHAMBERLAIN. I will, my lord.

        [He whispers to the Maskers.]

WOLSEY. What say they?

CHAMBERLAIN. Such a one, they all confess,
    There is indeed; which they would have your Grace
    Find out, and he will take it.

WOLSEY. Let me see, then. *[Comes from his state.]*
    By all your good leaves, gentlemen; here I'll make
    My royal choice.

KING. Ye have found him, Cardinal. *[Unmasking.]*
    You hold a fair assembly; you do well, lord.
    You are a churchman, or, I'll tell you, Cardinal,
    I should judge now unhappily.

WOLSEY. I am glad
    Your Grace is grown so pleasant.

KING. My Lord Chamberlain,
    Prithee come hither. What fair lady's that?

CHAMBERLAIN. An't please your Grace, Sir Thomas Bullen's daughter,—
    The Viscount Rochford—one of her Highness' women.

KING. By heaven, she is a dainty one. Sweetheart,
    I were unmannerly to take you out
    And not to kiss you. A health, gentlemen
    Let it go round.

WOLSEY. Sir Thomas Lovell, is the banquet ready
    I' the privy chamber?

LOVELL. Yes, my lord.

WOLSEY. Your Grace,
    I fear, with dancing is a little heated.

KING. I fear, too much.

WOLSEY. There's fresher air, my lord,
    In the next chamber.

KING. Lead in your ladies, every one. Sweet partner,
    I must not yet forsake you; let's be merry.
    Good my Lord Cardinal, I have half a dozen healths
    To drink to these fair ladies, and a measure
    To lead 'em once again; and then let's dream
    Who's best in favour. Let the music knock it.

                [Exeunt, with trumpets.]

ACT II.

SCENE I. *Westminster. A street.*

[*Enter two Gentlemen, at several doors.*]

FIRST GENTLEMAN. Whither away so fast?

SECOND GENTLEMAN. O, God save ye!
    Even to the hall, to hear what shall become
    Of the great Duke of Buckingham.

FIRST GENTLEMAN. I'll save you
    That labour, sir. All's now done, but the ceremony
    Of bringing back the prisoner.

SECOND GENTLEMAN. Were you there?

FIRST GENTLEMAN. Yes, indeed, was I.

SECOND GENTLEMAN. Pray, speak what has happen'd.

FIRST GENTLEMAN. You may guess quickly what.

SECOND GENTLEMAN. Is he found guilty?

FIRST GENTLEMAN. Yes, truly is he, and condemn'd upon't.

SECOND GENTLEMAN. I am sorry for't.

FIRST GENTLEMAN. So are a number more.

SECOND GENTLEMAN. But, pray, how pass'd it?

FIRST GENTLEMAN. I'll tell you in a little. The great Duke
    Came to the bar; where to his accusations
    He pleaded still not guilty and alleged
    Many sharp reasons to defeat the law.
    The King's attorney on the contrary
    Urg'd on the examinations, proofs, confessions
    Of divers witnesses; which the Duke desir'd
    To have brought viva voce to his face;
    At which appear'd against him his surveyor;
    Sir Gilbert Peck his chancellor; and John Car,
    Confessor to him, with that devil-monk,
    Hopkins, that made this mischief.

SECOND GENTLEMAN. That was he
That fed him with his prophecies?

FIRST GENTLEMAN. The same.
All these accus'd him strongly; which he fain
Would have flung from him, but, indeed, he could not.
And so his peers, upon this evidence,
Have found him guilty of high treason. Much
He spoke, and learnedly, for life; but all
Was either pitied in him or forgotten.

SECOND GENTLEMAN. After all this, how did he bear himself?

FIRST GENTLEMAN. When he was brought again to the bar, to hear
His knell rung out, his judgment, he was stirr'd
With such an agony, he sweat extremely,
And something spoke in choler, ill, and hasty.
But he fell to himself again, and sweetly
In all the rest show'd a most noble patience.

SECOND GENTLEMAN. I do not think he fears death.

FIRST GENTLEMAN. Sure, he does not;
He never was so womanish. The cause
He may a little grieve at.

SECOND GENTLEMAN. Certainly
The Cardinal is the end of this.

FIRST GENTLEMAN. 'Tis likely,
By all conjectures: first, Kildare's attainder,
Then deputy of Ireland; who remov'd,
Earl Surrey was sent thither, and in haste too,
Lest he should help his father.

SECOND GENTLEMAN. That trick of state
Was a deep envious one.

FIRST GENTLEMAN. At his return
No doubt he will requite it. This is noted,
And generally, whoever the King favours,
The Cardinal instantly will find employment,
And far enough from court too.

SECOND GENTLEMAN. All the commons
Hate him perniciously, and, o' my conscience,
Wish him ten fathom deep. This duke as much
They love and dote on; call him bounteous Buckingham,

The mirror of all courtesy,—

[*Enter BUCKINGHAM from his arraignment; Tip-staves before him; the axe with the edge towards him; halberds on each side; accompanied with SIR THOMAS LOVELL, SIR NICHOLAS VAUX, SIR WILLIAM SANDYS, and common people.*]

FIRST GENTLEMAN. Stay there, sir,
And see the noble ruin'd man you speak of.

SECOND GENTLEMAN. Let's stand close, and behold him.

BUCKINGHAM. All good people,
You that thus far have come to pity me,
Hear what I say, and then go home and lose me.
I have this day receiv'd a traitor's judgement,
And by that name must die; yet, Heaven bear witness,
And if I have a conscience, let it sink me,
Even as the axe falls, if I be not faithful!
The law I bear no malice for my death;
'T has done, upon the premises, but justice;
But those that sought it I could wish more Christians.
Be what they will, I heartily forgive 'em;
Yet let 'em look they glory not in mischief,
Nor build their evils on the graves of great men,
For then my guiltless blood must cry against 'em.
For further life in this world I ne'er hope,
Nor will I sue, although the King have mercies
More than I dare make faults. You few that lov'd me
And dare be bold to weep for Buckingham,
His noble friends and fellows, whom to leave
Is only bitter to him, only dying,
Go with me, like good angels, to my end;
And, as the long divorce of steel falls on me,
Make of your prayers one sweet sacrifice,
And lift my soul to heaven. Lead on, o' God's name.

LOVELL. I do beseech your Grace, for charity,
If ever any malice in your heart
Were hid against me, now to forgive me frankly.

BUCKINGHAM. Sir Thomas Lovell, I as free forgive you
As I would be forgiven. I forgive all.
There cannot be those numberless offences
'Gainst me, that I cannot take peace with; no black envy
Shall mark my grave. Commend me to his Grace;
And, if he speak of Buckingham, pray, tell him
You met him half in heaven. My vows and prayers

Yet are the King's; and, till my soul forsake,
Shall cry for blessings on him. May he live
Longer than I have time to tell his years!
Ever belov'd and loving may his rule be!
And when old Time shall lead him to his end,
Goodness and he fill up one monument!

LOVELL. To the water side I must conduct your Grace;
    Then give my charge up to Sir Nicholas Vaux,
    Who undertakes you to your end.

VAUX. Prepare there,
    The Duke is coming. See the barge be ready;
    And fit it with such furniture as suits
    The greatness of his person.

BUCKINGHAM. Nay, Sir Nicholas,
    Let it alone; my state now will but mock me.
    When I came hither, I was Lord High Constable
    And Duke of Buckingham; now, poor Edward Bohun.
    Yet I am richer than my base accusers,
    That never knew what truth meant. I now seal it;
    And with that blood will make 'em one day groan for't.
    My noble father, Henry of Buckingham,
    Who first rais'd head against usurping Richard,
    Flying for succour to his servant Banister,
    Being distress'd, was by that wretch betray'd,
    And without trial fell; God's peace be with him!
    Henry the Seventh succeeding, truly pitying
    My father's loss, like a most royal prince,
    Restor'd me to my honours, and, out of ruins,
    Made my name once more noble. Now his son,
    Henry the Eighth, life, honour, name, and all
    That made me happy, at one stroke has taken
    For ever from the world. I had my trial,
    And, must needs say, a noble one; which makes me
    A little happier than my wretched father.
    Yet thus far we are one in fortunes: both
    Fell by our servants, by those men we lov'd most;
    A most unnatural and faithless service.
    Heaven has an end in all; yet, you that hear me,
    This from a dying man receive as certain:
    Where you are liberal of your loves and counsels
    Be sure you be not loose; for those you make friends
    And give your hearts to, when they once perceive
    The least rub in your fortunes, fall away
    Like water from ye; never found again
    But where they mean to sink ye. All good people,

Pray for me! I must now forsake ye. The last hour
Of my long weary life is come upon me.
Farewell!
And when you would say something that is sad,
Speak how I fell. I have done; and God forgive me!

[*Exeunt Buckingham and Train.*]

FIRST GENTLEMAN. O, this is full of pity! Sir, it calls,
I fear, too many curses on their heads
That were the authors.

SECOND GENTLEMAN. If the Duke be guiltless,
'Tis full of woe; yet I can give you inkling
Of an ensuing evil, if it fall,
Greater than this.

FIRST GENTLEMAN. Good angels keep it from us!
What may it be? You do not doubt my faith, sir?

SECOND GENTLEMAN. This secret is so weighty, 'twill require
A strong faith to conceal it.

FIRST GENTLEMAN. Let me have it.
I do not talk much.

SECOND GENTLEMAN. I am confident;
You shall, sir. Did you not of late days hear
A buzzing of a separation
Between the King and Katherine?

FIRST GENTLEMAN. Yes, but it held not;
For when the King once heard it, out of anger
He sent command to the Lord Mayor straight
To stop the rumour, and allay those tongues
That durst disperse it.

SECOND GENTLEMAN. But that slander, sir,
Is found a truth now; for it grows again
Fresher than e'er it was; and held for certain
The King will venture at it. Either the Cardinal,
Or some about him near, have, out of malice
To the good Queen, possess'd him with a scruple
That will undo her. To confirm this too,
Cardinal Campeius is arriv'd, and lately;
As all think, for this business.

FIRST GENTLEMAN. 'Tis the Cardinal;
    And merely to revenge him on the Emperor
    For not bestowing on him, at his asking,
    The archbishopric of Toledo, this is purpos'd.

SECOND GENTLEMAN. I think you have hit the mark; but is't not cruel
    That she should feel the smart of this? The Cardinal
    Will have his will, and she must fall.

FIRST GENTLEMAN. 'Tis woeful.
    We are too open here to argue this;
    Let's think in private more.

[Exeunt.]

SCENE II. *London. The palace.*

[Enter the Lord Chamberlain, reading this letter.]

CHAMBERLAIN. "My lord, the horses your lordship sent for, with all the care had, I saw well chosen, ridden, and furnish'd. They were young and handsome, and of the best breed in the north. When they were ready to set out for London, a man of my Lord Cardinal's, by commission and main power, took 'em from me, with this reason: His master would be serv'd before a subject, if not before the King; which stopp'd our mouths, sir." I fear he will indeed. Well, let him have them:
    He will have all, I think.

[Enter to the Lord Chamberlain the DUKES OF NORFOLK and SUFFOLK.]

NORFOLK. Well met, my Lord Chamberlain.

CHAMBERLAIN. Good day to both your Graces.

SUFFOLK. How is the King employ'd?

CHAMBERLAIN. I left him private,
    Full of sad thoughts and troubles.

NORFOLK. What's the cause?

CHAMBERLAIN. It seems the marriage with his brother's wife
    Has crept too near his conscience.

SUFFOLK. No, his conscience
    Has crept too near another lady.

NORFOLK. 'Tis so.
    This is the Cardinal's doing, the king-cardinal.
    That blind priest, like the eldest son of Fortune,
    Turns what he list. The King will know him one day.

SUFFOLK. Pray God he do! he'll never know himself else.

NORFOLK. How holily he works in all his business!
    And with what zeal! for, now he has crack'd the league
    Between us and the Emperor, the Queen's great nephew,
    He dives into the King's soul, and there scatters
    Dangers, doubts, wringing of the conscience,
    Fears, and despairs; and all these for his marriage.
    And out of all these to restore the King,
    He counsels a divorce; a loss of her
    That, like a jewel, has hung twenty years
    About his neck, yet never lost her lustre;
    Of her that loves him with that excellence
    That angels love good men with; even of her
    That, when the greatest stroke of fortune falls,
    Will bless the King. And is not this course pious?

CHAMBERLAIN. Heaven keep me from such counsel! 'Tis most true
    These news are everywhere; every tongue speaks 'em,
    And every true heart weeps for't. All that dare
    Look into these affairs see this main end,
    The French king's sister. Heaven will one day open
    The King's eyes, that so long have slept upon
    This bold bad man.

SUFFOLK. And free us from his slavery.

NORFOLK. We had need pray,
    And heartily, for our deliverance;
    Or this imperious man will work us an
    From princes into pages. All men's honours
    Lie like one lump before him, to be fashion'd
    Into what pitch he please.

SUFFOLK. For me, my lords,
    I love him not, nor fear him; there's my creed.
    As I am made without him, so I'll stand,
    If the King please; his curses and his blessings
    Touch me alike, th'are breath I not believe in.
    I knew him, and I know him; so I leave him
    To him that made him proud, the Pope.

NORFOLK. Let's in;
>And with some other business put the King
>From these sad thoughts, that work too much upon him.
>My lord, you'll bear us company?

CHAMBERLAIN. Excuse me,
>The King has sent me otherwhere. Besides,
>You'll find a most unfit time to disturb him.
>Health to your lordships!

NORFOLK. Thanks, my good Lord Chamberlain.

>[*Exit Lord Chamberlain; and the King draws the curtain and sits reading
>pensively.*]

SUFFOLK. How sad he looks! Sure, he is much afflicted.

KING. Who's there, ha?

NORFOLK. Pray God he be not angry.

KING. Who's there, I say? How dare you thrust yourselves
>Into my private meditations?
>Who am I? ha?

NORFOLK. A gracious king that pardons all offences
>Malice ne'er meant. Our breach of duty this way
>Is business of estate; in which we come
>To know your royal pleasure.

KING. Ye are too bold.
>Go to; I'll make ye know your times of business.
>Is this an hour for temporal affairs, ha?

>[*Enter WOLSEY and CAMPEIUS, with a commission.*]

>Who's there? My good Lord Cardinal? O my Wolsey,
>The quiet of my wounded conscience,
>Thou art a cure fit for a King. [*To Campeius*] You're welcome,
>Most learned reverend sir, into our kingdom;
>Use us and it. [*To Wolsey*] My good lord, have great care
>I be not found a talker.

WOLSEY. Sir, you cannot.
>I would your Grace would give us but an hour
>Of private conference.

KING. [*To Norfolk and Suffolk*] We are busy; go.

NORFOLK. [*Aside to Suffolk*] This priest has no pride in him?

SUFFOLK. [*Aside to Norfolk*] Not to speak of.
    I would not be so sick, though, for his place.
    But this cannot continue.

NORFOLK. [*Aside to Suffolk*] If it do,
    I'll venture one have-at-him.

SUFFOLK. [*Aside to Norfolk*] I another.

            [*Exeunt Norfolk and Suffolk.*]

WOLSEY. Your Grace has given a precedent of wisdom
    Above all princes, in committing freely
    Your scruple to the voice of Christendom.
    Who can be angry now? What envy reach you?
    The Spaniard, tied by blood and favour to her,
    Must now confess, if they have any goodness,
    The trial just and noble. All the clerks,
    I mean the learned ones, in Christian kingdoms
    Have their free voices. Rome, the nurse of judgement,
    Invited by your noble self, hath sent
    One general tongue unto us, this good man,
    This just and learned priest, Cardinal Campeius,
    Whom once more I present unto your Highness.

KING. And once more in mine arms I bid him welcome,
    And thank the holy conclave for their loves.
    They have sent me such a man I would have wish'd for.

CAMPEIUS. Your Grace must needs deserve all strangers' loves,
    You are so noble. To your Highness' hand
    I tender my commission; by whose virtue,
    The court of Rome commanding—you, my Lord
    Cardinal of York, are join'd with me their servant
    In the unpartial judging of this business.

KING. Two equal men. The Queen shall be acquainted
    Forthwith for what you come. Where's Gardiner?

WOLSEY. I know your Majesty has always lov'd her
    So dear in heart not to deny her that
    A woman of less place might ask by law,
    Scholars allow'd freely to argue for her.

KING. Ay, and the best she shall have; and my favour
　　To him that does best; God forbid else. Cardinal,
　　Prithee, call Gardiner to me, my new secretary.
　　I find him a fit fellow.

[Exit Wolsey.]

[Re-enter WOLSEY with GARDINER.]

WOLSEY. [*Aside to Gardiner*]
　　Give me your hand. Much joy and favour to you;
　　You are the King's now.

GARDINER. [*Aside to Wolsey*] But to be commanded
　　For ever by your Grace, whose hand has rais'd me.

KING. Come hither, Gardiner.

[Walks and whispers.]

CAMPEIUS. My Lord of York, was not one Doctor Pace
　　In this man's place before him?

WOLSEY. Yes, he was.

CAMPEIUS. Was he not held a learned man?

WOLSEY. Yes, surely.

CAMPEIUS. Believe me, there's an ill opinion spread then
　　Even of yourself, Lord Cardinal.

WOLSEY. How! of me?

CAMPEIUS. They will not stick to say you envied him,
　　And fearing he would rise, he was so virtuous,
　　Kept him a foreign man still; which so griev'd him
　　That he ran mad and died.

WOLSEY. Heav'n's peace be with him!
　　That's Christian care enough. For living murmurers
　　There's places of rebuke. He was a fool,
　　For he would needs be virtuous. That good fellow,
　　If I command him, follows my appointment;
　　I will have none so near else. Learn this, brother,
　　We live not to be grip'd by meaner persons.

KING. Deliver this with modesty to the Queen.

[Exit Gardiner.]

The most convenient place that I can think of
For such receipt of learning is Black-Friars;
There ye shall meet about this weighty business.
My Wolsey, see it furnish'd. O, my lord,
Would it not grieve an able man to leave
So sweet a bedfellow? But, conscience, conscience!
O, 'tis a tender place; and I must leave her.

[Exeunt.]

SCENE III. *An ante-chamber of the Queen's apartments.*

[Enter ANNE BULLEN and an old Lady.]

ANNE. Not for that neither. Here's the pang that pinches:
　　His Highness having liv'd so long with her, and she
　　So good a lady that no tongue could ever
　　Pronounce dishonour of her,—by my life,
　　She never knew harm-doing—O, now, after
　　So many courses of the sun enthroned,
　　Still growing in a majesty and pomp, the which
　　To leave a thousand-fold more bitter than
　　'Tis sweet at first to acquire,—after this process,
　　To give her the avaunt, it is a pity
　　Would move a monster.

OLD LADY. Hearts of most hard temper
　　Melt and lament for her.

ANNE. O, God's will, much better
　　She ne'er had known pomp! Though't be temporal,
　　Yet, if that quarrel, fortune, do divorce
　　It from the bearer, 'tis a sufferance panging
　　As soul and body's severing.

OLD LADY. Alas, poor lady!
　　She's a stranger now again.

ANNE. So much the more
　　Must pity drop upon her. Verily,
　　I swear, 'tis better to be lowly born
　　And range with humble livers in content,
　　Than to be perk'd up in a glist'ring grief,
　　And wear a golden sorrow.

OLD LADY. Our content
    Is our best having.

ANNE. By my troth and maidenhead,
    I would not be a queen.

OLD LADY. Beshrew me, I would,
    And venture maidenhead for't; and so would you,
    For all this spice of your hypocrisy.
    You, that have so fair parts of woman on you,
    Have too a woman's heart, which ever yet
    Affected eminence, wealth, sovereignty;
    Which, to say sooth, are blessings; and which gifts,
    Saving your mincing, the capacity
    Of your soft cheveril conscience would receive,
    If you might please to stretch it.

ANNE. Nay, good troth.

OLD LADY. Yes, troth and troth. You would not be a queen?

ANNE. No, not for all the riches under heaven.

OLD LADY. 'Tis strange. A three-pence bow'd would hire me,
    Old as I am, to queen it. But, I pray you,
    What think you of a duchess? Have you limbs
    To bear that load of title?

ANNE. No, in truth.

OLD LADY. Then you are weakly made; pluck off a little.
    I would not be a young count in your way,
    For more than blushing comes to. If your back
    Cannot vouchsafe this burden, 'tis too weak
    Ever to get a boy.

ANNE. How you do talk!
    I swear again I would not be a queen
    For all the world.

OLD LADY. In faith, for little England
    You'd venture an emballing. I myself
    Would for Carnarvonshire, although there long'd
    No more to the crown but that. Lo, who comes here?

        [Enter the Lord Chamberlain.]

CHAMBERLAIN. Good morrow, ladies. What were't worth to know
    The secret of your conference?

ANNE. My good lord,
    Not your demand; it values not your asking.
    Our mistress' sorrows we were pitying.

CHAMBERLAIN. It was a gentle business, and becoming
    The action of good women. There is hope
    All will be well.

ANNE. Now, I pray God, amen!

CHAMBERLAIN. You bear a gentle mind, and heavenly blessings
    Follow such creatures. That you may, fair lady,
    Perceive I speak sincerely, and high note's
    Ta'en of your many virtues, the King's Majesty
    Commends his good opinion of you, and
    Does purpose honour to you no less flowing
    Than Marchioness of Pembroke; to which title
    A thousand pound a year, annual support,
    Out of his grace he adds.

ANNE. I do not know
    What kind of my obedience I should tender.
    More than my all is nothing; nor my prayers
    Are not words duly hallowed, nor my wishes
    More worth than empty vanities; yet prayers and wishes
    Are all I can return. Beseech your lordship,
    Vouchsafe to speak my thanks and my obedience,
    As from a blushing handmaid, to his Highness;
    Whose health and royalty I pray for.

CHAMBERLAIN. Lady,
    I shall not fail to approve the fair conceit
    The King hath of you. [*Aside*] I have perus'd her well.
    Beauty and honour in her are so mingled
    That they have caught the King; and who knows yet
    But from this lady may proceed a gem
    To lighten all this isle? I'll to the King,
    And say I spoke with you.

              [*Exit Lord Chamberlain.*]

ANNE. My honour'd lord.

OLD LADY. Why, this it is: see, see!
    I have been begging sixteen years in court,
    Am yet a courtier beggarly, nor could
    Come pat betwixt too early and too late
    For any suit of pounds; and you, O fate!
    A very fresh-fish here—fie, fie, fie upon
    This compell'd fortune!—have your mouth fill'd up
    Before you open it.

ANNE. This is strange to me.

OLD LADY. How tastes it? Is it bitter? Forty pence, no.
    There was a lady once, 'tis an old story,
    That would not be a queen, that would she not,
    For all the mud in Egypt. Have you heard it?

ANNE. Come, you are pleasant.

OLD LADY. With your theme, I could
    O'ermount the lark. The Marchioness of Pembroke!
    A thousand pounds a year for pure respect!
    No other obligation! By my life,
    That promises moe thousands: honour's train
    Is longer than his foreskirt. By this time
    I know your back will bear a duchess. Say,
    Are you not stronger than you were?

ANNE. Good lady,
    Make yourself mirth with your particular fancy,
    And leave me out on't. Would I had no being,
    If this salute my blood a jot. It faints me,
    To think what follows.
    The Queen is comfortless, and we forgetful
    In our long absence. Pray, do not deliver
    What here you've heard to her.

OLD LADY. What do you think me?

                 [*Exeunt.*]

SCENE IV. *London. A hall in Black-Friars.*

[*Trumpets, sennet, and cornets. Enter two Vergers, with short silver wands; next them, two Scribes, in the habit of doctors; after them, the ARCHBISHOP OF CANTERBURY alone; after him, the BISHOPS OF LINCOLN, ELY, ROCHESTER, and SAINT ASAPH; next them, with some small distance, follows a Gentleman bearing the purse, with the great seal, and a Cardinal's hat; then two Priests, bearing each silver cross; then a Gentleman Usher bareheaded, accompanied with a Sergeant-at-Arms bearing a silver mace; then two Gentlemen bearing two great silver pillars; after them, side by side, the two Cardinals; WOLSEY and CAMPEIUS; two Noblemen with the sword and mace. Then enter the KING and QUEEN and their Trains. The King takes place under the cloth of state; the two Cardinals sit under him as judges. The Queen takes place some distance from the King. The Bishops place themselves on each side the court, in manner of consistory; below them, the Scribes. The Lords sit next the Bishops. The rest of the Attendants stand in convenient order about the stage.*]

WOLSEY. Whilst our commission from Rome is read,
    Let silence be commanded.

KING. What's the need?
    It hath already publicly been read,
    And on all sides the authority allow'd;
    You may, then, spare that time.

WOLSEY. Be't so. Proceed.

SCRIBE. Say, Henry King of England, come into the court.

CRIER. Henry King of England, etc.

KING. Here.

SCRIBE. Say, Katherine Queen of England, come into the court.

CRIER. Katherine Queen of England, etc.

[*The Queen makes no answer, rises out of her chair, goes about the court, comes to the King, and kneels at his feet; then speaks.*]

QUEEN KATHERINE. Sir, I desire you do me right and justice,
    And to bestow your pity on me; for
    I am a most poor woman, and a stranger,
    Born out of your dominions, having here
    No judge indifferent, nor no more assurance

Of equal friendship and proceeding. Alas, sir,
In what have I offended you? What cause
Hath my behaviour given to your displeasure,
That thus you should proceed to put me off
And take your good grace from me? Heaven witness,
I have been to you a true and humble wife,
At all times to your will conformable;
Ever in fear to kindle your dislike,
Yea, subject to your countenance, glad or sorry
As I saw it inclin'd. When was the hour
I ever contradicted your desire,
Or made it not mine too? Or which of your friends
Have I not strove to love, although I knew
He were mine enemy? What friend of mine
That had to him deriv'd your anger, did I
Continue in my liking? Nay, gave notice
He was from thence discharg'd? Sir, call to mind
That I have been your wife in this obedience
Upward of twenty years, and have been blest
With many children by you. If, in the course
And process of this time, you can report,
And prove it too, against mine honour aught,
My bond to wedlock, or my love and duty,
Against your sacred person, in God's name,
Turn me away; and let the foul'st contempt
Shut door upon me, and so give me up
To the sharp'st kind of justice. Please you, sir,
The King, your father, was reputed for
A prince most prudent, of an excellent
And unmatch'd wit and judgment; Ferdinand,
My father, King of Spain, was reckon'd one
The wisest prince that there had reign'd by many
A year before; it is not to be question'd
That they had gather'd a wise council to them
Of every realm, that did debate this business,
Who deem'd our marriage lawful; wherefore I humbly
Beseech you, sir, to spare me till I may
Be by my friends in Spain advis'd, whose counsel
I will implore. If not, i' the name of God,
Your pleasure be fulfill'd!

WOLSEY. You have here, lady,
    And of your choice, these reverend fathers; men
    Of singular integrity and learning,
    Yea, the elect o' the land, who are assembled
    To plead your cause. It shall be therefore bootless
    That longer you desire the court; as well
    For your own quiet, as to rectify

What is unsettled in the King.

CAMPEIUS. His Grace
Hath spoken well and justly; therefore, madam,
It's fit this royal session do proceed,
And that, without delay, their arguments
Be now produc'd and heard.

QUEEN KATHERINE. Lord Cardinal,
To you I speak.

WOLSEY. Your pleasure, madam?

QUEEN KATHERINE. Sir,
I am about to weep; but, thinking that
We are a queen, or long have dream'd so, certain
The daughter of a king, my drops of tears
I'll turn to sparks of fire.

WOLSEY. Be patient yet.

QUEEN KATHERINE. I will, when you are humble; nay, before,
Or God will punish me. I do believe,
Induced by potent circumstances, that
You are mine enemy, and make my challenge
You shall not be my judge; for it is you
Have blown this coal betwixt my lord and me,
Which God's dew quench! Therefore I say again,
I utterly abhor, yea, from my soul
Refuse you for my judge; whom, yet once more,
I hold my most malicious foe, and think not
At all a friend to truth.

WOLSEY. I do profess
You speak not like yourself, who ever yet
Have stood to charity and display'd the effects
Of disposition gentle, and of wisdom
O'ertopping woman's pow'r. Madam, you do me wrong.
I have no spleen against you, nor injustice
For you or any. How far I have proceeded,
Or how far further shall, is warranted
By a commission from the consistory,
Yea, the whole consistory of Rome. You charge me
That I have blown this coal. I do deny it.
The King is present: if it be known to him
That I gainsay my deed, how may he wound,
And worthily, my falsehood! yea, as much
As you have done my truth. If he know

That I am free of your report, he knows
I am not of your wrong. Therefore in him
It lies to cure me; and the cure is, to
Remove these thoughts from you; the which before
His Highness shall speak in, I do beseech
You, gracious madam, to unthink your speaking
And to say so no more.

QUEEN KATHERINE. My lord, my lord,
　　I am a simple woman, much too weak
　　To oppose your cunning. You're meek and humble-mouth'd;
　　You sign your place and calling, in full seeming,
　　With meekness and humility; but your heart
　　Is cramm'd with arrogancy, spleen, and pride.
　　You have, by fortune and his Highness' favours,
　　Gone slightly o'er low steps and now are mounted
　　Where powers are your retainers, and your words,
　　Domestics to you, serve your will as 't please
　　Yourself pronounce their office. I must tell you,
　　You tender more your person's honour than
　　Your high profession spiritual; that again
　　I do refuse you for my judge; and here,
　　Before you all, appeal unto the Pope,
　　To bring my whole cause 'fore his Holiness,
　　And to be judg'd by him.

[She curtsies to the King, and offers to depart.]

CAMPEIUS. The Queen is obstinate,
　　Stubborn to justice, apt to accuse it, and
　　Disdainful to be tried by't; 'tis not well.
　　She's going away.

KING. Call her again.

CRIER. Katherine Queen of England, come into the court.

GENTLEMAN USHER. Madam, you are call'd back.

QUEEN KATHERINE. What need you note it? Pray you keep your way;
　　When you are call'd, return. Now, the Lord help!
　　They vex me past my patience. Pray you, pass on.
　　I will not tarry; no, nor ever more
　　Upon this business my appearance make
　　In any of their courts.

[Exeunt Queen, and her Attendants.]

KING. Go thy ways, Kate.
    That man i' the world who shall report he has
    A better wife, let him in nought be trusted,
    For speaking false in that. Thou art, alone,
    If thy rare qualities, sweet gentleness,
    Thy meekness saint-like, wife-like government,
    Obeying in commanding, and thy parts
    Sovereign and pious else, could speak thee out,
    The queen of earthly queens. She's noble born;
    And, like her true nobility, she has
    Carried herself towards me.

WOLSEY. Most gracious sir,
    In humblest manner I require your Highness,
    That it shall please you to declare, in hearing
    Of all these ears,—for, where I am robb'd and bound,
    There must I be unloos'd, although not there
    At once and fully satisfied,—whether ever I
    Did broach this business to your Highness, or
    Laid any scruple in your way, which might
    Induce you to the question on't, or ever
    Have to you, but with thanks to God for such
    A royal lady, spake one the least word that might
    Be to the prejudice of her present state,
    Or touch of her good person?

KING. My Lord Cardinal,
    I do excuse you; yea, upon mine honour,
    I free you from't. You are not to be taught
    That you have many enemies, that know not
    Why they are so, but, like to village-curs,
    Bark when their fellows do: by some of these
    The Queen is put in anger. You're excus'd;
    But will you be more justified? You ever
    Have wish'd the sleeping of this business; never desir'd
    It to be stirr'd; but oft have hind'red, oft,
    The passages made toward it. On my honour,
    I speak my good Lord Cardinal to this point,
    And thus far clear him. Now, what mov'd me to't,
    I will be bold with time and your attention:
    Then mark the inducement. Thus it came; give heed to't:
    My conscience first receiv'd a tenderness,
    Scruple, and prick, on certain speeches utter'd
    By the Bishop of Bayonne, then French ambassador;
    Who had been hither sent on the debating
    A marriage 'twixt the Duke of Orleans and
    Our daughter Mary. I' the progress of this business,
    Ere a determinate resolution, he,

I mean the Bishop, did require a respite;
Wherein he might the King his lord advertise
Whether our daughter were legitimate,
Respecting this our marriage with the dowager,
Sometimes our brother's wife. This respite shook
The bosom of my conscience, enter'd me,
Yea, with a splitting power, and made to tremble
The region of my breast; which forc'd such way,
That many maz'd considerings did throng
And press'd in with this caution. First, methought
I stood not in the smile of Heaven; who had
Commanded nature, that my lady's womb,
If it conceiv'd a male child by me, should
Do no more offices of life to't than
The grave does to the dead; for her male issue
Or died where they were made, or shortly after
This world had air'd them. Hence I took a thought
This was a judgement on me; that my kingdom,
Well worthy the best heir o' the world, should not
Be gladded in't by me. Then follows, that
I weigh'd the danger which my realms stood in
By this my issue's fail; and that gave to me
Many a groaning throe. Thus hulling in
The wild sea of my conscience, I did steer
Toward this remedy, whereupon we are
Now present here together; that's to say,
I meant to rectify my conscience, which
I then did feel full sick, and yet not well,
By all the reverend fathers of the land
And doctors learn'd. First I began in private
With you, my Lord of Lincoln. You remember
How under my oppression I did reek,
When I first mov'd you.

LINCOLN. Very well, my liege.

KING. I have spoke long; be pleas'd yourself to say
    How far you satisfied me.

LINCOLN. So please your Highness,
    The question did at first so stagger me,
    Bearing a state of mighty moment in't
    And consequence of dread, that I committed
    The daring'st counsel which I had to doubt;
    And did entreat your Highness to this course
    Which you are running here.

KING. I then mov'd you,
    My Lord of Canterbury; and got your leave
    To make this present summons. Unsolicited
    I left no reverend person in this court;
    But by particular consent proceeded
    Under your hands and seals. Therefore, go on;
    For no dislike i' the world against the person
    Of the good queen, but the sharp thorny points
    Of my alleged reasons, drives this forward.
    Prove but our marriage lawful, by my life
    And kingly dignity, we are contented
    To wear our mortal state to come with her,
    Katherine our queen, before the primest creature
    That's paragon'd o' the world.

CAMPEIUS. So please your Highness,
    The Queen being absent, 'tis a needful fitness
    That we adjourn this court till further day.
    Meanwhile must be an earnest motion
    Made to the Queen, to call back her appeal
    She intends unto his Holiness.

KING. [*Aside*] I may perceive
    These Cardinals trifle with me; I abhor
    This dilatory sloth and tricks of Rome.
    My learn'd and well-beloved servant, Cranmer,
    Prithee, return. With thy approach, I know,
    My comfort comes along.—Break up the court!
    I say, set on.

             [*Exeunt in manner as they enter'd.*]

ACT III.

SCENE I. *London. The Queen's apartments.*

[*The Queen and her Women, as at work.*]

QUEEN KATHERINE. Take thy lute, wench; my soul grows sad with troubles.
Sing, and disperse 'em, if thou canst. Leave working.

SONG

Orpheus with his lute made trees
And the mountain tops that freeze
Bow themselves when he did sing.
To his music plants and flowers
Ever sprung; as sun and showers
There had made a lasting spring.
Every thing that heard him play,
Even the billows of the sea,
Hung their heads, and then lay by.
In sweet music is such art,
Killing care and grief of heart
Fall asleep, or hearing, die.

[*Enter a Gentleman.*]

QUEEN KATHERINE. How now!

GENTLEMAN. An't please your Grace, the two great Cardinals
Wait in the presence.

QUEEN KATHERINE. Would they speak with me?

GENTLEMAN. They will'd me say so, madam.

QUEEN KATHERINE. Pray their Graces
To come near. [*Exit Gentleman.*] What can be their business
With me, a poor weak woman, fallen from favour?
I do not like their coming. Now I think on't,
They should be good men, their affairs as righteous.
But all hoods make not monks.

[*Enter the two Cardinals, WOLSEY and CAMPEIUS.*]

WOLSEY. Peace to your Highness!

QUEEN KATHERINE. Your Graces find me here part of housewife;
 I would be all, against the worst may happen.
 What are your pleasures with me, reverend lords?

WOLSEY. May it please you, noble madam, to withdraw
 Into your private chamber, we shall give you
 The full cause of our coming.

QUEEN KATHERINE. Speak it here;
 There's nothing I have done yet, o' my conscience,
 Deserves a corner. Would all other women
 Could speak this with as free a soul as I do!
 My lords, I care not, so much I am happy
 Above a number, if my actions
 Were tried by every tongue, every eye saw 'em,
 Envy and base opinion set against 'em,
 I know my life so even. If your business
 Seek me out, and that way I am wife in,
 Out with it boldly. Truth loves open dealing.

WOLSEY. Tanta est erga te mentis integritas, regina serenissima,—

QUEEN KATHERINE. O, good my lord, no Latin;
 I am not such a truant since my coming,
 As not to know the language I have liv'd in.
 A strange tongue makes my cause more strange, suspicious;
 Pray, speak in English. Here are some will thank you,
 If you speak truth, for their poor mistress' sake.
 Believe me, she has had much wrong. Lord Cardinal,
 The willing'st sin I ever yet committed
 May be absolv'd in English.

WOLSEY. Noble lady,
 I am sorry my integrity should breed,
 And service to his Majesty and you,
 So deep suspicion, where all faith was meant.
 We come not by the way of accusation
 To taint that honour every good tongue blesses,
 Nor to betray you any way to sorrow;
 You have too much, good lady; but to know
 How you stand minded in the weighty difference
 Between the King and you; and to deliver,
 Like free and honest men, our just opinions
 And comforts to your cause.

CAMPEIUS. Most honour'd madam,
    My Lord of York, out of his noble nature,
    Zeal and obedience he still bore your Grace,
    Forgetting, like a good man, your late censure
    Both of his truth and him, which was too far,
    Offers, as I do, in a sign of peace,
    His service and his counsel.

QUEEN KATHERINE. [*Aside*] To betray me.—
    My lords, I thank you both for your good wills.
    Ye speak like honest men; pray God, ye prove so!
    But how to make ye suddenly an answer,
    In such a point of weight, so near mine honour,—
    More near my life, I fear,—with my weak wit,
    And to such men of gravity and learning,
    In truth I know not. I was set at work
    Among my maids; full little, God knows, looking
    Either for such men or such business.
    For her sake that I have been,—for I feel
    The last fit of my greatness—good your Graces,
    Let me have time and counsel for my cause.
    Alas, I am a woman, friendless, hopeless!

WOLSEY. Madam, you wrong the King's love with these fears.
    Your hopes and friends are infinite.

QUEEN KATHERINE. In England
    But little for my profit. Can you think, lords,
    That any Englishman dare give me counsel?
    Or be a known friend, 'gainst his Highness' pleasure,
    Though he be grown so desperate to be honest,
    And live a subject? Nay, forsooth; my friends,
    They that much weigh out my afflictions,
    They that my trust must grow to, live not here;
    They are, as all my other comforts, far hence
    In mine own country, lords.

CAMPEIUS. I would your Grace
    Would leave your griefs, and take my counsel.

QUEEN KATHERINE. How, sir?

CAMPEIUS. Put your main cause into the King's protection;
    He's loving and most gracious. 'Twill be much
    Both for your honour better and your cause;
    For if the trial of the law o'ertake ye,
    You'll part away disgrac'd.

WOLSEY. He tells you rightly.

QUEEN KATHERINE. Ye tell me what ye wish for both,—my ruin.
Is this your Christian counsel? Out upon ye!
Heaven is above all yet; there sits a judge
That no king can corrupt.

CAMPEIUS. Your rage mistakes us.

QUEEN KATHERINE. The more shame for ye! Holy men I thought ye,
Upon my soul, two reverend cardinal virtues;
But cardinal sins and hollow hearts I fear ye.
Mend 'em, for shame, my lords! Is this your comfort,
The cordial that ye bring a wretched lady,
A woman lost among ye, laugh'd at, scorn'd?
I will not wish ye half my miseries;
I have more charity; but say, I warn'd ye.
Take heed, for heaven's sake, take heed, lest at once
The burden of my sorrows fall upon ye.

WOLSEY. Madam, this is a mere distraction;
You turn the good we offer into envy.

QUEEN KATHERINE. Ye turn me into nothing. Woe upon ye
And all such false professors! Would you have me—
If you have any justice, any pity;
If ye be anything but churchmen's habits—
Put my sick cause into his hands that hates me?
Alas! has banish'd me his bed already,
His love, too, long ago! I am old, my lords,
And all the fellowship I hold now with him
Is only my obedience. What can happen
To me above this wretchedness? All your studies
Make me a curse like this.

CAMPEIUS. Your fears are worse.

QUEEN KATHERINE. Have I liv'd thus long—let me speak myself,
Since virtue finds no friends—a wife, a true one?
A woman, I dare say without vain-glory,
Never yet branded with suspicion?
Have I with all my full affections
Still met the King, lov'd him next Heav'n, obey'd him?
Been, out of fondness, superstitious to him?
Almost forgot my prayers to content him?
And am I thus rewarded! 'Tis not well, lords.
Bring me a constant woman to her husband,

One that ne'er dream'd a joy beyond his pleasure;
And to that woman, when she has done most,
Yet will I add an honour,—a great patience.

WOLSEY. Madam, you wander from the good we aim at.

QUEEN KATHERINE. My lord, I dare not make myself so guilty,
To give up willingly that noble title
Your master wed me to. Nothing but death
Shall e'er divorce my dignities.

WOLSEY. Pray hear me.

QUEEN KATHERINE. Would I had never trod this English earth,
Or felt the flatteries that grow upon it!
Ye have angels' faces, but Heaven knows your hearts.
What will become of me now, wretched lady!
I am the most unhappy woman living.
[*To her Women*] Alas, poor wenches, where are now your fortunes!
Shipwreck'd upon a kingdom, where no pity,
No friends, no hope; no kindred weep for me;
Almost no grave allow'd me. Like the lily,
That once was mistress of the field and flourish'd,
I'll hang my head and perish.

WOLSEY. If your Grace
Could but be brought to know our ends are honest,
You'd feel more comfort. Why should we, good lady,
Upon what cause, wrong you? Alas, our places,
The way of our profession is against it;
We are to cure such sorrows, not to sow 'em.
For goodness' sake, consider what you do;
How you may hurt yourself, ay, utterly
Grow from the King's acquaintance, by this carriage.
The hearts of princes kiss obedience,
So much they love it; but to stubborn spirits
They swell, and grow as terrible as storms.
I know you have a gentle, noble temper,
A soul as even as a calm; pray, think us
Those we profess, peacemakers, friends, and servants.

CAMPEIUS. Madam, you'll find it so. You wrong your virtues
With these weak women's fears. A noble spirit
As yours was, put into you, ever casts
Such doubts, as false coin, from it. The King loves you;
Beware you lose it not. For us, if you please
To trust us in your business, we are ready
To use our utmost studies in your service.

QUEEN KATHERINE. Do what ye will, my lords; and, pray, forgive me
    If I have us'd myself unmannerly;
    You know I am a woman, lacking wit
    To make a seemly answer to such persons.
    Pray, do my service to his Majesty;
    He has my heart yet, and shall have my prayers
    While I shall have my life. Come, reverend fathers,
    Bestow your counsels on me. She now begs,
    That little thought, when she set footing here,
    She should have bought her dignities so dear.

[Exeunt.]

SCENE II. *London. The palace.*

[*Enter the DUKE OF NORFOLK, the DUKE OF SUFFOLK, the EARL OF SURREY, and the Lord Chamberlain.*]

NORFOLK. If you will now unite in your complaints
    And force them with a constancy, the Cardinal
    Cannot stand under them. If you omit
    The offer of this time, I cannot promise
    But that you shall sustain moe new disgraces,
    With these you bear already.

SURREY. I am joyful
    To meet the least occasion that may give me
    Remembrance of my father-in-law, the Duke,
    To be reveng'd on him.

SUFFOLK. Which of the peers
    Have uncontemn'd gone by him, or at least
    Strangely neglected? When did he regard
    The stamp of nobleness in any person
    Out of himself?

CHAMBERLAIN. My lords, you speak your pleasures.
    What he deserves of you and me I know;
    What we can do to him, though now the time
    Gives way to us, I much fear. If you cannot
    Bar his access to the King, never attempt
    Anything on him; for he hath a witchcraft
    Over the King in 's tongue.

NORFOLK. O, fear him not;
    His spell in that is out. The King hath found
    Matter against him that for ever mars
    The honey of his language. No, he's settled,
    Not to come off, in his displeasure.

SURREY. Sir,
    I should be glad to hear such news as this
    Once every hour.

NORFOLK. Believe it, this is true.
    In the divorce his contrary proceedings
    Are all unfolded; wherein he appears
    As I would wish mine enemy.

SURREY. How came
    His practices to light?

SUFFOLK. Most strangely.

SURREY. O, how, how?

SUFFOLK. The Cardinal's letters to the Pope miscarried,
    And came to the eye o' the King; wherein was read,
    How that the Cardinal did entreat his Holiness
    To stay the judgement o' the divorce; for if
    It did take place, "I do" quoth he "perceive
    My king is tangled in affection to
    A creature of the Queen's, Lady Anne Bullen."

SURREY. Has the King this?

SUFFOLK. Believe it.

SURREY. Will this work?

CHAMBERLAIN. The King in this perceives him, how he coasts
    And hedges his own way. But in this point
    All his tricks founder, and he brings his physic
    After his patient's death. The King already
    Hath married the fair lady.

SURREY. Would he had!

SUFFOLK. May you be happy in your wish, my lord!
    For, I profess, you have it.

SURREY. Now, all my joy
    Trace the conjunction!

SUFFOLK. My amen to't!

NORFOLK. All men's!

SUFFOLK. There's order given for her coronation.
    Marry, this is yet but young, and may be left
    To some ears unrecounted. But, my lords,
    She is a gallant creature, and complete
    In mind and feature. I persuade me, from her
    Will fall some blessing to this land, which shall
    In it be memoriz'd.

SURREY. But, will the King
    Digest this letter of the Cardinal's?
    The Lord forbid!

NORFOLK. Marry, amen!

SUFFOLK. No, no;
    There be moe wasps that buzz about his nose
    Will make this sting the sooner. Cardinal Campeius
    Is stolen away to Rome; hath ta'en no leave;
    He's left the cause o' the King unhandled, and
    Is posted, as the agent of our Cardinal,
    To second all his plot. I do assure you
    The King cried "Ha!" at this.

CHAMBERLAIN. Now, God incense him,
    And let him cry "Ha!" louder!

NORFOLK. But, my lord,
    When returns Cranmer?

SUFFOLK. He is return'd in his opinions; which
    Have satisfied the King for his divorce,
    Together with all famous colleges
    Almost in Christendom. Shortly, I believe,
    His second marriage shall be publish'd, and
    Her coronation. Katherine no more
    Shall be call'd Queen, but Princess Dowager
    And widow to Prince Arthur.

NORFOLK. This same Cranmer's
    A worthy fellow, and hath ta'en much pain
    In the King's business.

SUFFOLK. He has; and we shall see him
    For it an archbishop.

NORFOLK. So I hear.

SUFFOLK. 'Tis so.

          [Enter WOLSEY and CROMWELL.]

    The Cardinal!

NORFOLK. Observe, observe, he's moody.

WOLSEY. The packet, Cromwell,
    Gave't you the King?

CROMWELL. To his own hand, in 's bedchamber.

WOLSEY. Look'd he o' the inside of the paper?

CROMWELL. Presently
    He did unseal them; and the first he view'd,
    He did it with a serious mind; a heed
    Was in his countenance. You he bade
    Attend him here this morning.

WOLSEY. Is he ready
    To come abroad?

CROMWELL. I think, by this he is.

WOLSEY. Leave me awhile.

          [Exit Cromwell.]

    [Aside.] It shall be to the Duchess of Alençon,
    The French king's sister; he shall marry her.
    Anne Bullen! No; I'll no Anne Bullens for him;
    There's more in't than fair visage. Bullen!
    No, we'll no Bullens. Speedily I wish
    To hear from Rome. The Marchioness of Pembroke!

NORFOLK. He's discontented.

SUFFOLK. May be, he hears the King
    Does whet his anger to him.

SURREY. Sharp enough,
    Lord, for thy justice!

WOLSEY. [*Aside.*] The late queen's gentlewoman, a knight's daughter,
    To be her mistress' mistress! the Queen's queen!
    This candle burns not clear: 'tis I must snuff it;
    Then out it goes. What though I know her virtuous
    And well deserving? yet I know her for
    A spleeny Lutheran; and not wholesome to
    Our cause, that she should lie i' the bosom of
    Our hard-rul'd King. Again, there is sprung up
    An heretic, an arch one, Cranmer; one
    Hath crawl'd into the favour of the King,
    And is his oracle.

NORFOLK. He's vex'd at something.

        [*Enter the KING, reading a schedule, and LOVELL.*]

SURREY. I would 'twere something that would fret the string,
    The master-cord on 's heart!

SUFFOLK. The King, the King!

KING. What piles of wealth hath he accumulated
    To his own portion! And what expense by the hour
    Seems to flow from him! How, i' the name of thrift,
    Does he rake this together! Now, my lords,
    Saw you the Cardinal?

NORFOLK. My lord, we have
    Stood here observing him. Some strange commotion
    Is in his brain; he bites his lip, and starts;
    Stops on a sudden, looks upon the ground,
    Then lays his finger on his temple; straight
    Springs out into fast gait; then stops again,
    Strikes his breast hard; and anon he casts
    His eye against the moon. In most strange postures
    We have seen him set himself.

KING. It may well be;
    There is a mutiny in 's mind. This morning
    Papers of state he sent me to peruse,
    As I requir'd; and wot you what I found
    There,—on my conscience, put unwittingly?
    Forsooth, an inventory, thus importing
    The several parcels of his plate, his treasure,
    Rich stuffs, and ornaments of household; which

I find at such proud rate, that it out-speaks
Possession of a subject.

NORFOLK. It's Heaven's will!
    Some spirit put this paper in the packet,
    To bless your eye withal.

KING. If we did think
    His contemplation were above the earth ,
    And fix'd on spiritual object, he should still
    Dwell in his musings; but I am afraid
    His thinkings are below the moon, not worth
    His serious considering.

[*The King takes his seat and whispers Lovell, who goes to the Cardinal.*]

WOLSEY. Heaven forgive me!
    Ever God bless your Highness!

KING. Good my lord,
    You are full of heavenly stuff, and bear the inventory
    Of your best graces in your mind; the which
    You were now running o'er. You have scarce time
    To steal from spiritual leisure a brief span
    To keep your earthly audit. Sure, in that
    I deem you an ill husband, and am glad
    To have you therein my companion.

WOLSEY. Sir,
    For holy offices I have a time; a time
    To think upon the part of business which
    I bear i' the state; and Nature does require
    Her times of preservation, which perforce
    I, her frail son, amongst my brethren mortal,
    Must give my tendance to.

KING. You have said well.

WOLSEY. And ever may your Highness yoke together,
    As I will lend you cause, my doing well
    With my well saying!

KING. 'Tis well said again;
    And 'tis a kind of good deed to say well;
    And yet words are no deeds. My father lov'd you;
    He said he did; and with his deed did crown
    His word upon you. Since I had my office,
    I have kept you next my heart; have not alone

    Employ'd you where high profits might come home,
    But par'd my present havings, to bestow
    My bounties upon you.

WOLSEY. [*Aside*] What should this mean?

SURREY. [*Aside*] The Lord increase this business!

KING. Have I not made you
    The prime man of the state? I pray you, tell me,
    If what I now pronounce you have found true
    And, if you may confess it, say withal,
    If you are bound to us or no. What say you?

WOLSEY. My sovereign, I confess your royal graces,
    Show'r'd on me daily, have been more than could
    My studied purposes requite, which went
    Beyond all man's endeavours. My endeavours
    Have ever come too short of my desires,
    Yet fil'd with my abilities. Mine own ends
    Have been mine so that evermore they pointed
    To the good of your most sacred person and
    The profit of the state. For your great graces
    Heap'd upon me, poor undeserver, I
    Can nothing render but allegiant thanks,
    My prayers to heaven for you, my loyalty,
    Which ever has and ever shall be growing,
    Till death, that winter, kill it.

KING. Fairly answer'd.
    A loyal and obedient subject is
    Therein illustrated. The honour of it
    Does pay the act of it, as i' the contrary,
    The foulness is the punishment. I presume
    That, as my hand has open'd bounty to you,
    My heart dropp'd love, my pow'r rain'd honour, more
    On you than any, so your hand and heart,
    Your brain, and every function of your power,
    Should, notwithstanding that your bond of duty,
    As 'twere in love's particular, be more
    To me, your friend, than any.

WOLSEY. I do profess
    That for your Highness' good I ever labour'd
    More than mine own, that am, have, and will be—
    Though all the world should crack their duty to you,
    And throw it from their soul; though perils did
    Abound, as thick as thought could make 'em, and

Appear in forms more horrid,—yet my duty,
As doth a rock against the chiding flood,
Should the approach of this wild river break,
And stand unshaken yours.

KING. 'Tis nobly spoken.
Take notice, lords, he has a loyal breast,
For you have seen him open't. Read o'er this;

[*Giving him papers.*]

And, after, this; and then to breakfast with
What appetite you have.

[*Exit King, frowning upon Cardinal; the Nobles throng after him, smiling and whispering.*]

WOLSEY. What should this mean?
What sudden anger's this? How have I reap'd it?
He parted frowning from me, as if ruin
Leap'd from his eyes. So looks the chafed lion
Upon the daring huntsman that has gall'd him;
Then makes him nothing. I must read this paper;
I fear, the story of his anger. 'Tis so;
This paper has undone me. 'Tis the account
Of all that world of wealth I have drawn together
For mine own ends; indeed, to gain the popedom
And fee my friends in Rome. O negligence,
Fit for a fool to fall by! What cross devil
Made me put this main secret in the packet
I sent the King? Is there no way to cure this?
No new device to beat this from his brains?
I know 'twill stir him strongly; yet I know
A way, if it take right, in spite of fortune,
Will bring me off again. What's this? "To the Pope!"
The letter, as I live, with all the business
I writ to 's Holiness. Nay then, farewell!
I have touch'd the highest point of all my greatness;
And from that full meridian of my glory,
I haste now to my setting. I shall fall
Like a bright exhalation in the evening,
And no man see me more.

[*Re-enter to Wolsey, the DUKES OF NORFOLK and SUFFOLK, the EARL OF SURREY, and the Lord Chamberlain.*]

NORFOLK. Hear the King's pleasure, Cardinal, who commands you
    To render up the great seal presently
    Into our hands; and to confine yourself
    To Asher House, my Lord of Winchester's,
    Till you hear further from his Highness.

WOLSEY. Stay!
    Where's your commission, lords? Words cannot carry
    Authority so weighty.

SUFFOLK. Who dares cross 'em,
    Bearing the King's will from his mouth expressly?

WOLSEY. Till I find more than will or words to do it,
    I mean your malice, know, officious lords,
    I dare and must deny it. Now I feel
    Of what coarse metal ye are moulded, envy.
    How eagerly ye follow my disgraces,
    As if it fed ye! and how sleek and wanton
    Ye appear in every thing may bring my ruin!
    Follow your envious courses, men of malice!
    You have Christian warrant for 'em, and, no doubt,
    In time will find their fit rewards. That seal
    You ask with such a violence, the King,
    Mine and your master, with his own hand gave me,
    Bade me enjoy it, with the place and honours,
    During my life; and, to confirm his goodness,
    Tied it by letters-patents. Now, who'll take it?

SURREY. The King, that gave it.

WOLSEY. It must be himself, then.

SURREY. Thou art a proud traitor, priest.

WOLSEY. Proud lord, thou liest!
    Within these forty hours Surrey durst better
    Have burnt that tongue than said so.

SURREY. Thy ambition,
    Thou scarlet sin, robb'd this bewailing land
    Of noble Buckingham, my father-in-law.
    The heads of all thy brother cardinals,
    With thee and all thy best parts bound together,
    Weigh'd not a hair of his. Plague of your policy!
    You sent me deputy for Ireland,
    Far from his succour, from the King, from all

That might have mercy on the fault thou gav'st him;
Whilst your great goodness, out of holy pity,
Absolv'd him with an axe.

WOLSEY. This, and all else
This talking lord can lay upon my credit,
I answer is most false. The Duke by law
Found his deserts. How innocent I was
From any private malice in his end,
His noble jury and foul cause can witness.
If I lov'd many words, lord, I should tell you
You have as little honesty as honour,
That in the way of loyalty and truth
Toward the King, my ever royal master,
Dare mate a sounder man than Surrey can be
And all that love his follies.

SURREY. By my soul,
Your long coat, priest, protects you; thou shouldst feel
My sword i' the life-blood of thee else. My lords,
Can ye endure to hear this arrogance?
And from this fellow? If we live thus tamely,
To be thus jaded by a piece of scarlet,
Farewell nobility! Let his Grace go forward
And dare us with his cap like larks.

WOLSEY. All goodness
Is poison to thy stomach.

SURREY. Yes, that goodness
Of gleaning all the land's wealth into one,
Into your own hands, Cardinal, by extortion;
The goodness of your intercepted packets
You writ to the Pope against the King. Your goodness,
Since you provoke me, shall be most notorious.
My Lord of Norfolk, as you are truly noble,
As you respect the common good, the state
Of our despis'd nobility, our issues,
Who, if he live, will scarce be gentlemen,
Produce the grand sum of his sins, the articles
Collected from his life. I'll startle you
Worse than the sacring bell, when the brown wench
Lay kissing in your arms, Lord Cardinal.

WOLSEY. How much, methinks, I could despise this man,
But that I am bound in charity against it!

NORFOLK. Those articles, my lord, are in the King's hand:
    But, thus much, they are foul ones.

WOLSEY. So much fairer
    And spotless shall mine innocence arise,
    When the King knows my truth.

SURREY. This cannot save you.
    I thank my memory, I yet remember
    Some of these articles; and out they shall.
    Now, if you can blush and cry "guilty," Cardinal,
    You'll show a little honesty.

WOLSEY. Speak on, sir;
    I dare your worst objections. If I blush,
    It is to see a nobleman want manners.

SURREY. I had rather want those than my head. Have at you!
    First, that, without the King's assent or knowledge,
    You wrought to be a legate; by which power
    You maim'd the jurisdiction of all bishops.

NORFOLK. Then, that in all you writ to Rome, or else
    To foreign princes, "Ego et Rex meus"
    Was still inscrib'd; in which you brought the King
    To be your servant.

SUFFOLK. Then, that, without the knowledge
    Either of king or council, when you went
    Ambassador to the Emperor, you made bold
    To carry into Flanders the great seal.

SURREY. Item, you sent a large commission
    To Gregory de Cassado, to conclude,
    Without the King's will or the state's allowance,
    A league between his Highness and Ferrara.

SUFFOLK. That, out of mere ambition, you have caus'd
    Your holy hat to be stamp'd on the King's coin.

SURREY. Then, that you have sent innumerable substance,
    By what means got, I leave to your own conscience,
    To furnish Rome, and to prepare the ways
    You have for dignities; to the mere undoing
    Of all the kingdom. Many more there are;
    Which, since they are of you, and odious,
    I will not taint my mouth with.

CHAMBERLAIN. O my lord,
 Press not a falling man too far! 'tis virtue.
 His faults lie open to the laws; let them,
 Not you, correct him. My heart weeps to see him
 So little of his great self.

SURREY. I forgive him.

SUFFOLK. Lord Cardinal, the King's further pleasure is,
 Because all those things you have done of late
 By your power legatine within this kingdom,
 Fall into the compass of a praemunire,
 That therefore such a writ be sued against you;
 To forfeit all your goods, lands, tenements,
 Chattels, and whatsoever, and to be
 Out of the King's protection. This is my charge.

NORFOLK. And so we'll leave you to your meditations
 How to live better. For your stubborn answer
 About the giving back the great seal to us,
 The King shall know it, and, no doubt, shall thank you.
 So fare you well, my little good Lord Cardinal.

     [Exeunt all but Wolsey.]

WOLSEY. So farewell to the little good you bear me.
 Farewell! a long farewell, to all my greatness!
 This is the state of man: to-day he puts forth
 The tender leaves of hopes; to-morrow blossoms,
 And bears his blushing honours thick upon him;
 The third day comes a frost, a killing frost,
 And, when he thinks, good easy man, full surely
 His greatness is a-ripening, nips his root,
 And then he falls, as I do. I have ventur'd,
 Like little wanton boys that swim on bladders,
 This many summers in a sea of glory,
 But far beyond my depth. My high-blown pride
 At length broke under me, and now has left me,
 Weary and old with service, to the mercy
 Of a rude stream, that must for ever hide me.
 Vain pomp and glory of this world, I hate ye!
 I feel my heart new open'd. O, how wretched
 Is that poor man that hangs on princes' favours!
 There is, betwixt that smile we would aspire to,
 That sweet aspect of princes, and their ruin,
 More pangs and fears than wars or women have;
 And when he falls, he falls like Lucifer,

Never to hope again.

[*Enter CROMWELL, standing amazed.*]

Why, how now, Cromwell!

CROMWELL. I have no power to speak, sir.

WOLSEY. What, amaz'd
　　At my misfortunes? Can thy spirit wonder
　　A great man should decline? Nay, an you weep,
　　I am fallen indeed.

CROMWELL. How does your Grace?

WOLSEY. Why, well,
　　Never so truly happy, my good Cromwell.
　　I know myself now; and I feel within me
　　A peace above all earthly dignities,
　　A still and quiet conscience. The King has cur'd me,
　　I humbly thank his Grace; and from these shoulders,
　　These ruin'd pillars, out of pity, taken
　　A load would sink a navy, too much honour.
　　O, 'tis a burden, Cromwell, 'tis a burden
　　Too heavy for a man that hopes for heaven!

CROMWELL. I am glad your Grace has made that right use of it.

WOLSEY. I hope I have. I am able now, methinks,
　　Out of a fortitude of soul I feel,
　　To endure more miseries and greater far
　　Than my weak-hearted enemies dare offer.
　　What news abroad?

CROMWELL. The heaviest and the worst
　　Is your displeasure with the King.

WOLSEY. God bless him!

CROMWELL. The next is, that Sir Thomas More is chosen
　　Lord Chancellor in your place.

WOLSEY. That's somewhat sudden;
　　But he's a learned man. May he continue
　　Long in his Highness' favour, and do justice
　　For truth's sake and his conscience; that his bones,
　　When he has run his course and sleeps in blessings,
　　May have a tomb of orphans' tears wept on 'em!

What more?

CROMWELL. That Cranmer is return'd with welcome,
    Install'd Lord Archbishop of Canterbury.

WOLSEY. That's news indeed.

CROMWELL. Last, that the Lady Anne,
    Whom the King hath in secrecy long married,
    This day was view'd in open as his queen,
    Going to chapel; and the voice is now
    Only about her coronation.

WOLSEY. There was the weight that pull'd me down. O Cromwell,
    The King has gone beyond me! All my glories
    In that one woman I have lost for ever.
    No sun shall ever usher forth mine honours,
    Or gild again the noble troops that waited
    Upon my smiles. Go, get thee from me, Cromwell!
    I am a poor fallen man, unworthy now
    To be thy lord and master. Seek the King!
    That sun, I pray, may never set! I have told him
    What and how true thou art. He will advance thee;
    Some little memory of me will stir him—
    I know his noble nature—not to let
    Thy hopeful service perish too. Good Cromwell,
    Neglect him not; make use now, and provide
    For thine own future safety.

CROMWELL. O my lord,
    Must I, then, leave you? Must I needs forgo
    So good, so noble, and so true a master?
    Bear witness, all that have not hearts of iron,
    With what a sorrow Cromwell leaves his lord.
    The King shall have my service; but my prayers
    For ever and for ever shall be yours.

WOLSEY. Cromwell, I did not think to shed a tear
    In all my miseries; but thou hast forc'd me,
    Out of thy honest truth, to play the woman.
    Let's dry our eyes; and thus far hear me, Cromwell;
    And when I am forgotten, as I shall be,
    And sleep in dull cold marble, where no mention
    Of me more must be heard of, say, I taught thee;
    Say, Wolsey, that once trod the ways of glory,
    And sounded all the depths and shoals of honour,
    Found thee a way, out of his wreck, to rise in;
    A sure and safe one, though thy master miss'd it.

Mark but my fall, and that that ruin'd me.
Cromwell, I charge thee, fling away ambition!
By that sin fell the angels; how can man, then,
The image of his Maker, hope to win by it?
Love thyself last. Cherish those hearts that hate thee;
Corruption wins not more than honesty.
Still in thy right hand carry gentle peace,
To silence envious tongues. Be just, and fear not;
Let all the ends thou aim'st at be thy country's,
Thy God's, and truth's; then if thou fall'st, O Cromwell,
Thou fall'st a blessed martyr!
Serve the King!—And, prithee, lead me in.
There take an inventory of all I have,
To the last penny; 'tis the King's. My robe,
And my integrity to Heaven, is all
I dare now call mine own. O Cromwell, Cromwell!
Had I but serv'd my God with half the zeal
I serv'd my king, He would not in mine age
Have left me naked to mine enemies.

CROMWELL. Good sir, have patience.

WOLSEY. So I have. Farewell
  The hopes of court! My hopes in heaven do dwell.

[Exeunt.]

ACT IV.

SCENE I. *A street in Westminster.*

[*Enter two Gentlemen, meeting one another.*]

FIRST GENTLEMAN. You're well met once again.

SECOND GENTLEMAN. So are you.

FIRST GENTLEMAN. You come to take your stand here, and behold
    The Lady Anne pass from her coronation?

SECOND GENTLEMAN. 'Tis all my business. At our last encounter,
    The Duke of Buckingham came from his trial.

FIRST GENTLEMAN. 'Tis very true; but that time offer'd sorrow;
    This, general joy.

SECOND GENTLEMAN. 'Tis well. The citizens,
    I am sure, have shown at full their royal minds—
    As, let 'em have their rights, they are ever forward—
    In celebration of this day with shows,
    Pageants, and sights of honour.

FIRST GENTLEMAN. Never greater,
    Nor, I'll assure you, better taken, sir.

SECOND GENTLEMAN. May I be bold to ask what that contains,
    That paper in your hand?

FIRST GENTLEMAN. Yes; 'tis the list
    Of those that claim their offices this day
    By custom of the coronation.
    The Duke of Suffolk is the first, and claims
    To be High Steward; next, the Duke of Norfolk,
    He to be Earl Marshal. You may read the rest.

SECOND GENTLEMAN. I thank you, sir; had I not known those customs,
    I should have been beholding to your paper.
    But, I beseech you, what's become of Katherine,
    The Princess Dowager? How goes her business?

FIRST GENTLEMAN. That I can tell you too. The Archbishop
    Of Canterbury, accompanied with other
    Learned and reverend fathers of his order,
    Held a late court at Dunstable, six miles off
    From Ampthill where the Princess lay; to which
    She was often cited by them, but appear'd not;
    And, to be short, for not appearance and
    The King's late scruple, by the main assent
    Of all these learned men she was divorc'd,
    And the late marriage made of none effect;
    Since which she was remov'd to Kimbolton,
    Where she remains now sick.

SECOND GENTLEMAN. Alas, good lady!

[Trumpets.]

The trumpets sound; stand close, the Queen is coming.

[Hautboys.]

THE ORDER OF THE CORONATION.

1. *A lively flourish of trumpets.*
2. *Then, Two Judges.*
3. *Lord Chancellor, with purse and mace before him.*
4. *Choristers, singing. [Music.]*
5. *Mayor of London, bearing the mace. Then Garter, in his coat of arms, and on his head he wore a gilt copper crown.*
6. *MARQUIS DORSET, bearing a sceptre of gold, on his head a demi-coronal of gold. With him, the EARL OF SURREY, bearing the rod of silver with the dove, crowned with an earl's coronet. Collars of SS.*
7. *DUKE OF SUFFOLK, in his robe of estate, his coronet on his head, bearing a long white wand, as high steward. With him, The DUKE OF NORFOLK, with the rod of marshalship, a coronet on his head. Collars of SS.*
8. *A canopy borne by four of the CINQUEPORTS; under it, the QUEEN in her robe, in her hair richly adorned with pearl, crowned. On each side her, the Bishops of London and Winchester.*
9. *The old DUCHESS OF NORFOLK, in a coronal of gold, wrought with flowers, bearing the Queen's train.*
10. *Certain Ladies or Countesses, with plain circlets of gold without flowers.*

    [Exeunt, first passing over the stage in order and state, and then a great flourish of trumpets.]

SECOND GENTLEMAN. A royal train, believe me. These I know.
    Who's that that bears the sceptre?

FIRST GENTLEMAN. Marquis Dorset;
 And that the Earl of Surrey, with the rod.

SECOND GENTLEMAN. A bold brave gentleman. That should be
 The Duke of Suffolk?

FIRST GENTLEMAN. 'Tis the same: High Steward.

SECOND GENTLEMAN. And that my Lord of Norfolk?

FIRST GENTLEMAN. Yes.

SECOND GENTLEMAN. Heaven bless thee! [*Looking on the Queen.*]
 Thou hast the sweetest face I ever look'd on.
 Sir, as I have a soul, she is an angel;
 Our king has all the Indies in his arms,
 And more and richer, when he strains that lady.
 I cannot blame his conscience.

FIRST GENTLEMAN. They that bear
 The cloth of honour over her, are four barons
 Of the Cinque-ports.

SECOND GENTLEMAN. Those men are happy; and so are all are near her.
 I take it, she that carries up the train
 Is that old noble lady, Duchess of Norfolk.

FIRST GENTLEMAN. It is; and all the rest are countesses.

SECOND GENTLEMAN. Their coronets say so. These are stars indeed;
 And sometimes falling ones.

FIRST GENTLEMAN. No more of that.

    [*Exit Procession, with a great flourish of trumpets.*]

     [*Enter a third Gentleman.*]

God save you, sir! Where have you been broiling?

THIRD GENTLEMAN. Among the crowds i' the Abbey, where a finger
 Could not be wedg'd in more. I am stifled
 With the mere rankness of their joy.

SECOND GENTLEMAN. You saw the ceremony?

THIRD GENTLEMAN. That I did.

FIRST GENTLEMAN. How was it?

THIRD GENTLEMAN. Well worth the seeing.

SECOND GENTLEMAN. Good sir, speak it to us.

THIRD GENTLEMAN. As well as I am able. The rich stream
    Of lords and ladies, having brought the Queen
    To a prepar'd place in the choir, fell of
    A distance from her; while her Grace sat down
    To rest a while, some half an hour or so,
    In a rich chair of state, opposing freely
    The beauty of her person to the people,—
    Believe me, sir, she is the goodliest woman
    That ever lay by man;—which when the people
    Had the full view of, such a noise arose
    As the shrouds make at sea in a stiff tempest,
    As loud, and to as many tunes. Hats, cloaks,—
    Doublets, I think,—flew up; and had their faces
    Been loose, this day they had been lost. Such joy
    I never saw before. Great-bellied women,
    That had not half a week to go, like rams
    In the old time of war, would shake the press
    And make 'em reel before 'em. No man living
    Could say "This is my wife" there; all were woven
    So strangely in one piece.

SECOND GENTLEMAN. But what follow'd?

THIRD GENTLEMAN. At length her Grace rose, and with modest paces
    Came to the altar; where she kneel'd, and saintlike
    Cast her fair eyes to heaven and pray'd devoutly;
    Then rose again and bow'd her to the people,
    When by the Archbishop of Canterbury
    She had all the royal makings of a queen,
    As holy oil, Edward Confessor's crown,
    The rod, and bird of peace, and all such emblems
    Laid nobly on her; which perform'd, the choir,
    With all the choicest music of the kingdom,
    Together sung "Te Deum." So she parted,
    And with the same full state pac'd back again
    To York Place, where the feast is held.

FIRST GENTLEMAN. Sir,
    You must no more call it York Place, that's past;
    For, since the Cardinal fell, that title's lost.
    'Tis now the King's, and call'd Whitehall.

THIRD GENTLEMAN. I know it;
 But 'tis so lately alter'd, that the old name
 Is fresh about me.

SECOND GENTLEMAN. What two reverend bishops
 Were those that went on each side of the Queen?

THIRD GENTLEMAN. Stokesly and Gardiner; the one of Winchester,
 Newly preferr'd from the King's secretary;
 The other, London.

SECOND GENTLEMAN. He of Winchester
 Is held no great good lover of the Archbishop's,
 The virtuous Cranmer.

THIRD GENTLEMAN. All the land knows that.
 However, yet there is no great breach; when it comes,
 Cranmer will find a friend will not shrink from him.

SECOND GENTLEMAN. Who may that be, I pray you?

THIRD GENTLEMAN. Thomas Cromwell;
 A man in much esteem with the King, and truly
 A worthy friend. The King has made him master
 O' the jewel house,
 And one, already, of the privy council.

SECOND GENTLEMAN. He will deserve more.

THIRD GENTLEMAN. Yes, without all doubt.
 Come, gentlemen, ye shall go my way, which
 Is to the court, and there ye shall be my guests;
 Something I can command. As I walk thither,
 I'll tell ye more.

BOTH. You may command us, sir.

[Exeunt.]

SCENE II. *Kimbolton.*

[Enter KATHERINE, Dowager, sick; led between GRIFFITH, her Gentleman Usher, and PATIENCE, her woman.]

GRIFFITH. How does your Grace?

KATHERINE. O Griffith, sick to death!
    My legs, like loaden branches, bow to the earth,
    Willing to leave their burden. Reach a chair.
    So; now, methinks, I feel a little ease.
    Didst thou not tell me, Griffith, as thou led'st me,
    That the great child of honour, Cardinal Wolsey,
    Was dead?

GRIFFITH. Yes, madam; but I think your Grace,
    Out of the pain you suffer'd, gave no ear to't.

KATHERINE. Prithee, good Griffith, tell me how he died.
    If well, he stepp'd before me, happily
    For my example.

GRIFFITH. Well, the voice goes, madam:
    For after the stout Earl Northumberland
    Arrested him at York, and brought him forward,
    As a man sorely tainted, to his answer,
    He fell sick suddenly, and grew so ill
    He could not sit his mule.

KATHERINE. Alas, poor man!

GRIFFITH. At last, with easy roads, he came to Leicester,
    Lodg'd in the abbey; where the reverend abbot,
    With all his convent, honourably receiv'd him;
    To whom he gave these words: "O, father abbot,
    An old man, broken with the storms of state,
    Is come to lay his weary bones among ye;
    Give him a little earth for charity!"
    So went to bed, where eagerly his sickness
    Pursu'd him still; and, three nights after this,
    About the hour of eight, which he himself
    Foretold should be his last, full of repentance,
    Continual meditations, tears, and sorrows,
    He gave his honours to the world again,
    His blessed part to heaven, and slept in peace.

KATHERINE. So may he rest; his faults lie gently on him!
    Yet thus far, Griffith, give me leave to speak him,
    And yet with charity. He was a man
    Of an unbounded stomach, ever ranking
    Himself with princes; one that, by suggestion,
    Tied all the kingdom. Simony was fair-play;
    His own opinion was his law; i' the presence
    He would say untruths; and be ever double
    Both in his words and meaning. He was never,
    But where he meant to ruin, pitiful.
    His promises were, as he then was, mighty;
    But his performance, as he is now, nothing.
    Of his own body he was ill, and gave
    The clergy ill example.

GRIFFITH. Noble madam,
    Men's evil manners live in brass; their virtues
    We write in water. May it please your Highness
    To hear me speak his good now?

KATHERINE. Yes, good Griffith;
    I were malicious else.

GRIFFITH. This Cardinal,
    Though from an humble stock, undoubtedly
    Was fashion'd to much honour from his cradle.
    He was a scholar, and a ripe and good one;
    Exceeding wise, fair-spoken, and persuading;
    Lofty and sour to them that lov'd him not,
    But to those men that sought him, sweet as summer.
    And though he were unsatisfied in getting,
    Which was a sin, yet in bestowing, madam,
    He was most princely: ever witness for him
    Those twins of learning that he rais'd in you,
    Ipswich and Oxford! one of which fell with him,
    Unwilling to outlive the good that did it;
    The other, though unfinish'd, yet so famous,
    So excellent in art, and still so rising,
    That Christendom shall ever speak his virtue.
    His overthrow heap'd happiness upon him;
    For then, and not till then, he felt himself,
    And found the blessedness of being little;
    And, to add greater honours to his age
    Than man could give him, he died fearing God.

KATHERINE. After my death I wish no other herald,
No other speaker of my living actions,
To keep mine honour from corruption,
But such an honest chronicler as Griffith.
Whom I most hated living, thou hast made me,
With thy religious truth and modesty,
Now in his ashes honour. Peace be with him!
Patience, be near me still, and set me lower:
I have not long to trouble thee. Good Griffith,
Cause the musicians play me that sad note
I nam'd my knell, whilst I sit meditating
On that celestial harmony I go to.

[*Sad and solemn music.*]

GRIFFITH. She is asleep. Good wench, let's sit down quiet,
For fear we wake her; softly, gentle Patience.

THE VISION

[*Enter, solemnly tripping one after another, six personages, clad in white robes, wearing on their heads garlands of bays, and golden vizards on their faces; branches of bays or palm in their hands. They first congee unto her, then dance; and, at certain changes, the first two hold a spare garland over her head; at which the other four make reverent curtsies. Then the two that held the garland deliver the same to the other next two, who observe the same order in their changes, and holding the garland over her head; which done, they deliver the same garland to the last two, who likewise observe the same order; at which, as it were by inspiration, she makes in her sleep signs of rejoicing, and holdeth up her hands to heaven: and so in their dancing vanish, carrying the garland with them. The music continues.*]

KATHERINE. Spirits of peace, where are ye? Are ye all gone,
And leave me here in wretchedness behind ye?

GRIFFITH. Madam, we are here.

KATHERINE. It is not you I call for.
Saw ye none enter since I slept?

GRIFFITH. None, madam.

KATHERINE. No? Saw you not, even now, a blessed troop
Invite me to a banquet; whose bright faces
Cast thousand beams upon me, like the sun?
They promis'd me eternal happiness,
And brought me garlands, Griffith, which I feel

I am not worthy yet to wear. I shall, assuredly.

GRIFFITH. I am most joyful, madam, such good dreams
Possess your fancy.

KATHERINE. Bid the music leave,
They are harsh and heavy to me.

[*Music ceases.*]

PATIENCE. Do you note
How much her Grace is alter'd on the sudden?
How long her face is drawn! How pale she looks,
And of an earthly cold! Mark her eyes!

GRIFFITH. She is going, wench. Pray, pray.

PATIENCE. Heaven comfort her!

[*Enter a Messenger.*]

MESSENGER. An't like your Grace,—

KATHERINE. You are a saucy fellow.
Deserve we no more reverence?

GRIFFITH. You are to blame,
Knowing she will not lose her wonted greatness,
To use so rude behaviour. Go to, kneel.

MESSENGER. I humbly do entreat your Highness' pardon;
My haste made me unmannerly. There is staying
A gentleman, sent from the King, to see you.

KATHERINE. Admit him entrance, Griffith; but this fellow
Let me ne'er see again.

[*Exit Messenger.*]

[*Enter LORD CAPUCIUS.*]

If my sight fail not,
You should be lord ambassador from the Emperor,
My royal nephew, and your name Capucius.

CAPUCIUS. Madam, the same; your servant.

KATHERINE. O, my lord,
  The times and titles now are alter'd strangely
  With me since first you knew me. But, I pray you,
  What is your pleasure with me?

CAPUCIUS. Noble lady,
  First, mine own service to your Grace; the next,
  The King's request that I would visit you,
  Who grieves much for your weakness, and by me
  Sends you his princely commendations,
  And heartily entreats you take good comfort.

KATHERINE. O my good lord, that comfort comes too late;
  'Tis like a pardon after execution.
  That gentle physic, given in time, had cur'd me;
  But now I am past all comforts here, but prayers.
  How does his Highness?

CAPUCIUS. Madam, in good health.

KATHERINE. So may he ever do! and ever flourish,
  When I shall dwell with worms, and my poor name
  Banish'd the kingdom! Patience, is that letter,
  I caused you write, yet sent away?

PATIENCE. No, madam.

[*Giving it to Katherine.*]

KATHERINE. Sir, I most humbly pray you to deliver
  This to my lord the King.

CAPUCIUS. Most willing, madam.

KATHERINE. In which I have commended to his goodness
  The model of our chaste loves, his young daughter;
  The dews of heaven fall thick in blessings on her!
  Beseeching him to give her virtuous breeding,—
  She is young, and of a noble modest nature,
  I hope she will deserve well,—and a little
  To love her for her mother's sake, that lov'd him,
  Heaven knows how dearly. My next poor petition
  Is, that his noble Grace would have some pity
  Upon my wretched women, that so long
  Have follow'd both my fortunes faithfully;
  Of which there is not one, I dare avow,
  And now I should not lie, but will deserve,

For virtue and true beauty of the soul,
For honesty and decent carriage,
A right good husband; let him be a noble;
And, sure, those men are happy that shall have 'em.
The last is, for my men,—they are the poorest,
But poverty could never draw 'em from me—
That they may have their wages duly paid 'em,
And something over to remember me by.
If Heaven had pleas'd to have given me longer life
And able means, we had not parted thus.
These are the whole contents; and, good my lord,
By that you love the dearest in this world,
As you wish Christian peace to souls departed,
Stand these poor people's friend, and urge the King
To do me this last right.

CAPUCIUS. By heaven, I will,
    Or let me lose the fashion of a man!

KATHERINE. I thank you, honest lord. Remember me
    In all humility unto his Highness.
    Say his long trouble now is passing
    Out of this world; tell him, in death I bless'd him,
    For so I will. Mine eyes grow dim. Farewell,
    My lord. Griffith, farewell. Nay, Patience,
    You must not leave me yet. I must to bed;
    Call in more women. When I am dead, good wench,
    Let me be us'd with honour. Strew me over
    With maiden flowers, that all the world may know
    I was a chaste wife to my grave. Embalm me,
    Then lay me forth. Although unqueen'd, yet like
    A queen, and daughter to a king, inter me.
    I can no more.

[Exeunt, leading Katherine.]

ACT V.

SCENE I. *London. A gallery in the palace.*

[*Enter GARDINER, BISHOP OF WINCHESTER, a Page with a torch before him, met by SIR THOMAS LOVELL.*]

GARDINER. It's one o'clock, boy, is't not?

PAGE. It hath struck.

GARDINER. These should be hours for necessities,
Not for delights; times to repair our nature
With comforting repose, and not for us
To waste these times. Good hour of night, Sir Thomas!
Whither so late?

LOVELL. Came you from the King, my lord?

GARDINER. I did, Sir Thomas; and left him at primero
With the Duke of Suffolk.

LOVELL. I must to him too,
Before he go to bed. I'll take my leave.

GARDINER. Not yet, Sir Thomas Lovell. What's the matter?
It seems you are in haste. An if there be
No great offence belongs to't, give your friend
Some touch of your late business. Affairs, that walk,
As they say spirits do, at midnight, have
In them a wilder nature than the business
That seeks despatch by day.

LOVELL. My lord, I love you;
And durst commend a secret to your ear
Much weightier than this work. The Queen's in labour,
They say in great extremity; and fear'd
She'll with the labour end.

GARDINER. The fruit she goes with
I pray for heartily, that it may find
Good time, and live; but for the stock, Sir Thomas,
I wish it grubb'd up now.

LOVELL. Methinks I could
    Cry thee amen; and yet my conscience says
    She's a good creature, and, sweet lady, does
    Deserve our better wishes.

GARDINER. But, sir, sir,
    Hear me, Sir Thomas. You're a gentleman
    Of mine own way; I know you wise, religious;
    And, let me tell you, it will ne'er be well,
    'Twill not, Sir Thomas Lovell, take't of me,
    Till Cranmer, Cromwell, her two hands, and she,
    Sleep in their graves.

LOVELL. Now, sir, you speak of two
    The most remark'd i' the kingdom. As for Cromwell,
    Beside that of the jewel house, is made master
    O' the rolls, and the King's secretary; further, sir,
    Stands in the gap and trade of moe preferments,
    With which the time will load him. The Archbishop
    Is the King's hand and tongue; and who dare speak
    One syllable against him?

GARDINER. Yes, yes, Sir Thomas,
    There are that dare; and I myself have ventur'd
    To speak my mind of him: and indeed this day,
    Sir, I may tell it you, I think I have
    Incens'd the lords o' the council, that he is,
    For so I know he is, they know he is,
    A most arch heretic, a pestilence
    That does infect the land; with which they moved
    Have broken with the King, who hath so far
    Given ear to our complaint, of his great grace
    And princely care foreseeing those fell mischiefs
    Our reasons laid before him, hath commanded
    To-morrow morning to the council-board
    He be convented. He's a rank weed, Sir Thomas,
    And we must root him out. From your affairs
    I hinder you too long. Good-night, Sir Thomas.

LOVELL. Many good-nights, my lord! I rest your servant.

[*Exeunt Gardiner and Page.*]

[*Enter the KING and DUKE OF SUFFOLK.*]

KING. Charles, I will play no more to-night.
    My mind's not on't; you are too hard for me.

SUFFOLK. Sir, I did never win of you before.

KING. But little, Charles;
    Nor shall not, when my fancy's on my play.
    Now, Lovell, from the Queen what is the news?

LOVELL. I could not personally deliver to her
    What you commanded me, but by her woman
    I sent your message; who return'd her thanks
    In the great'st humbleness, and desir'd your Highness
    Most heartily to pray for her.

KING. What say'st thou, ha?
    To pray for her? What, is she crying out?

LOVELL. So said her woman; and that her suff'rance made
    Almost each pang a death.

KING. Alas, good lady!

SUFFOLK. God safely quit her of her burden, and
    With gentle travail, to the gladding of
    Your Highness with an heir!

KING. 'Tis midnight, Charles;
    Prithee, to bed; and in thy prayers remember
    The estate of my poor queen. Leave me alone;
    For I must think of that which company
    Will not be friendly to.

SUFFOLK. I wish your Highness
    A quiet night; and my good mistress will
    Remember in my prayers.

KING. Charles, good-night.

                [Exit Suffolk.]

          [Enter SIR ANTHONY DENNY.]

  Well, sir, what follows?

DENNY. Sir, I have brought my lord the Archbishop,
    As you commanded me.

KING. Ha! Canterbury?

DENNY. Ay, my good lord.

KING. 'Tis true; where is he, Denny?

DENNY. He attends your Highness' pleasure.

KING. Bring him to us.

[*Exit Denny.*]

LOVELL. [*Aside*] This is about that which the bishop spake.
 I am happily come hither.

[*Re-enter DENNY, with CRANMER.*]

KING. Avoid the gallery. [*Lovell seems to stay.*]
 Ha! I have said. Be gone.
 What!

[*Exeunt Lovell and Denny.*]

CRANMER. [*Aside*] I am fearful; wherefore frowns he thus?
 'Tis his aspect of terror. All's not well.

KING. How now, my lord! you do desire to know
 Wherefore I sent for you.

CRANMER. [*Kneeling*] It is my duty
 To attend your Highness' pleasure.

KING. Pray you, arise,
 My good and gracious Lord of Canterbury.
 Come, you and I must walk a turn together;
 I have news to tell you. Come, come, me your hand.
 Ah, my good lord, I grieve at what I speak,
 And am right sorry to repeat what follows.
 I have, and most unwillingly, of late
 Heard many grievous, I do say, my lord,
 Grievous complaints of you; which, being consider'd,
 Have mov'd us and our council, that you shall
 This morning come before us; where, I know,
 You cannot with such freedom purge yourself
 But that, till further trial in those charges
 Which will require your answer, you must take
 Your patience to you, and be well contented
 To make your house our Tower. You a brother of us,
 It fits we thus proceed, or else no witness
 Would come against you.

CRANMER. [*Kneeling*] I humbly thank your Highness;
    And am right glad to catch this good occasion
    Most throughly to be winnowed, where my chaff
    And corn shall fly asunder; for, I know,
    There's none stands under more calumnious tongues
    Than I myself, poor man.

KING. Stand up, good Canterbury!
    Thy truth and thy integrity is rooted
    In us, thy friend. Give me thy hand, stand up;
    Prithee, let's walk. Now, by my holidame,
    What manner of man are you? My lord, I look'd
    You would have given me your petition, that
    I should have ta'en some pains to bring together
    Yourself and your accusers; and to have heard you,
    Without indurance, further.

CRANMER. Most dread liege,
    The good I stand on is my truth and honesty.
    If they shall fail, I, with mine enemies,
    Will triumph o'er my person; which I weigh not,
    Being of those virtues vacant. I fear nothing
    What can be said against me.

KING. Know you not
    How your state stands i' th' world, with the whole world?
    Your enemies are many, and not small; their practices
    Must bear the same proportion; and not ever
    The justice and the truth o' the question carries
    The due o' the verdict with it. At what ease
    Might corrupt minds procure knaves as corrupt
    To swear against you? Such things have been done.
    You are potently oppos'd, and with a malice
    Of as great size. Ween you of better luck,
    I mean, in perjur'd witness, than your Master,
    Whose minister you are, whiles here He liv'd
    Upon this naughty earth? Go to, go to!
    You take a precipice for no leap of danger,
    And woo your own destruction.

CRANMER. God and your Majesty
    Protect mine innocence, or I fall into
    The trap is laid for me!

KING. Be of good cheer;
    They shall no more prevail than we give way to.
    Keep comfort to you; and this morning see
    You do appear before them. If they shall chance,
    In charging you with matters, to commit you,
    The best persuasions to the contrary
    Fail not to use, and with what vehemency
    The occasion shall instruct you. If entreaties
    Will render you no remedy, this ring
    Deliver them, and your appeal to us
    There make before them. Look, the good man weeps!
    He's honest, on mine honour. God's blest mother!
    I swear he is true-hearted; and a soul
    None better in my kingdom. Get you gone,
    And do as I have bid you.

[Exit Cranmer.]

He has strangled his language in his tears.

[Enter Old Lady.]

GENTLEMAN. [*Within.*] Come back! What mean you?

OLD LADY. I'll not come back; the tidings that I bring
    Will make my boldness manners. Now, good angels
    Fly o'er thy royal head, and shade thy person
    Under their blessed wings!

KING. Now, by thy looks
    I guess thy message. Is the Queen deliver'd?
    Say ay; and of a boy.

OLD LADY. Ay, ay, my liege;
    And of a lovely boy. The God of Heaven
    Both now and ever bless her! 'tis a girl,
    Promises boys hereafter. Sir, your queen
    Desires your visitation, and to be
    Acquainted with this stranger. 'Tis as like you
    As cherry is to cherry.

KING. Lovell!

[Enter LOVELL.]

LOVELL. Sir?

KING. Give her an hundred marks. I'll to the Queen. [*Exit*.]

OLD LADY. An hundred marks! By this light, I'll ha' more.
　　An ordinary groom is for such payment.
　　I will have more, or scold it out of him.
　　Said I for this, the girl was like to him?
　　I will have more, or else unsay't; and now,
　　While it is hot, I'll put it to the issue.

[*Exeunt*.]

SCENE II. *Lobby before the Council Chamber.*

[*Enter CRANMER, ARCHBISHOP OF CANTERBURY.*]

CRANMER. I hope I am not too late; and yet the gentleman,
　　That was sent to me from the council, pray'd me
　　To make great haste. All fast? what means this? Ho!
　　Who waits there? Sure, you know me?

[*Enter Keeper.*]

KEEPER. Yes, my lord;
　　But yet I cannot help you.

CRANMER. Why?

KEEPER. Your Grace must wait till you be call'd for.

[*Enter Doctor Butts.*]

CRANMER. So.

BUTTS. [*Aside*] This is a piece of malice. I am glad
　　I came this way so happily; the King
　　Shall understand it presently. [*Exit*.]

CRANMER. [*Aside*] 'Tis Butts,
　　The King's physician. As he pass'd along,
　　How earnestly he cast his eyes upon me!
　　Pray Heaven, he sound not my disgrace! For certain,
　　This is of purpose laid by some that hate me—
　　God turn their hearts! I never sought their malice—
　　To quench mine honour; they would shame to make me
　　Wait else at door, a fellow-counsellor,
　　'Mong boys, grooms, and lackeys. But their pleasures
　　Must be fulfill'd, and I attend with patience.

[Enter the KING and BUTTS, at a window above.]

BUTTS. I'll show your Grace the strangest sight—

KING. What's that, Butts?

BUTTS. I think your Highness saw this many a day.

KING. Body o' me, where is it?

BUTTS. There, my lord,
    The high promotion of his Grace of Canterbury;
    Who holds his state at door, 'mongst pursuivants,
    Pages, and footboys.

KING. Ha! 'tis he, indeed.
    Is this the honour they do one another?
    'Tis well there's one above 'em yet. I had thought
    They had parted so much honesty among 'em,
    At least, good manners, as not thus to suffer
    A man of his place, and so near our favour,
    To dance attendance on their lordships' pleasures,
    And at the door too, like a post with packets.
    By holy Mary, Butts, there's knavery.
    Let 'em alone, and draw the curtain close;
    We shall hear more anon.

[Exeunt.]

SCENE III. *The Council Chamber.*

[A council-table brought in with chairs and stools, and placed under the state. Enter Lord Chancellor; places himself at the upper end of the table on the left hand, a seat being left void above him, as for Canterbury's seat. DUKE OF SUFFOLK, DUKE OF NORFOLK, SURREY, LORD CHAMBERLAIN, GARDINER, seat themselves in order on each side. CROMWELL at lower end, as secretary. Keeper at the door.]

CHANCELLOR. Speak to the business, master secretary.
    Why are we met in council?

CROMWELL. Please your honours,
    The chief cause concerns his Grace of Canterbury.

GARDINER. Has he had knowledge of it?

CROMWELL. Yes.

NORFOLK. Who waits there?

KEEPER. Without, my noble lords?

GARDINER. Yes.

KEEPER. My Lord Archbishop;
    And has done half an hour, to know your pleasures.

CHANCELLOR. Let him come in.

KEEPER. Your Grace may enter now.

[*CRANMER approaches the Council table.*]

CHANCELLOR. My good Lord Archbishop, I'm very sorry
    To sit here at this present, and behold
    That chair stand empty; but we all are men,
    In our own natures frail, and capable
    Of our flesh; few are angels: out of which frailty
    And want of wisdom, you, that best should teach us,
    Have misdemean'd yourself, and not a little,
    Toward the King first, then his laws, in filling
    The whole realm, by your teaching and your chaplains,
    For so we are inform'd, with new opinions
    Divers and dangerous, which are heresies
    And, not reform'd, may prove pernicious.

GARDINER. Which reformation must be sudden too,
    My noble lords; for those that tame wild horses
    Pace 'em not in their hands to make 'em gentle,
    But stop their mouth with stubborn bits and spur 'em
    Till they obey the manage. If we suffer,
    Out of our easiness and childish pity
    To one man's honour, this contagious sickness,
    Farewell all physic! And what follows then?
    Commotions, uproars, with a general taint
    Of the whole state; as, of late days, our neighbours,
    The upper Germany, can dearly witness,
    Yet freshly pitied in our memories.

CRANMER. My good lords, hitherto in all the progress
    Both of my life and office, I have labour'd,
    And with no little study, that my teaching
    And the strong course of my authority
    Might go one way, and safely; and the end
    Was ever, to do well; nor is there living,
    I speak it with a single heart, my lords,

A man that more detests, more stirs against,
Both in his private conscience and his place,
Defacers of a public peace, than I do.
Pray Heaven, the King may never find a heart
With less allegiance in it! Men that make
Envy and crooked malice nourishment
Dare bite the best. I do beseech your lordships,
That, in this case of justice, my accusers,
Be what they will, may stand forth face to face
And freely urge against me.

SUFFOLK. Nay, my lord,
That cannot be. You are a counsellor,
And, by that virtue, no man dare accuse you.

GARDINER. My lord, because we have business of more moment,
We will be short with you. 'Tis his Highness' pleasure
And our consent, for better trial of you,
From hence you be committed to the Tower;
Where, being but a private man again,
You shall know many dare accuse you boldly,
More than, I fear, you are provided for.

CRANMER. Ah, my good Lord of Winchester, I thank you.
You are always my good friend; if your will pass,
I shall both find your lordship judge and juror,
You are so merciful. I see your end;
'Tis my undoing. Love and meekness, lord,
Become a churchman better than ambition.
Win straying souls with modesty again,
Cast none away. That I shall clear myself,
Lay all the weight ye can upon my patience,
I make as little doubt as you do conscience
In doing daily wrongs. I could say more,
But reverence to your calling makes me modest.

GARDINER. My lord, my lord, you are a sectary,
That's the plain truth. Your painted gloss discovers,
To men that understand you, words and weakness.

CROMWELL. My Lord of Winchester, you are a little,
By your good favour, too sharp; men so noble,
However faulty, yet should find respect
For what they have been. 'Tis a cruelty
To load a falling man.

GARDINER. Good master secretary,
    I cry your honour mercy. You may, worst
    Of all this table, say so.

CROMWELL. Why, my lord?

GARDINER. Do not I know you for a favourer
    Of this new sect? Ye are not sound.

CROMWELL. Not sound?

GARDINER. Not sound, I say.

CROMWELL. Would you were half so honest!
    Men's prayers then would seek you, not their fears.

GARDINER. I shall remember this bold language.

CROMWELL. Do.
    Remember your bold life too.

CHANCELLOR. This is too much.
    Forbear, for shame, my lords.

GARDINER. I have done.

CROMWELL. And I.

CHANCELLOR. Then thus for you, my lord: it stands agreed,
    I take it, by all voices, that forthwith
    You be convey'd to the Tower a prisoner;
    There to remain till the King's further pleasure
    Be known unto us. Are you all agreed, lords?

ALL. We are.

CRANMER. Is there no other way of mercy,
    But I must needs to the Tower, my lords?

GARDINER. What other
    Would you expect? You are strangely troublesome.
    Let some o' the guard be ready there.

                    [Enter the Guard.]

CRANMER. For me?
    Must I go like a traitor thither?

GARDINER. Receive him,
    And see him safe i' the Tower.

CRANMER. Stay, good my lords,
    I have a little yet to say. Look there, my lords;
    By virtue of that ring, I take my cause
    Out of the gripes of cruel men, and give it
    To a most noble judge, the King my master.

CHAMBERLAIN. This is the King's ring.

SURREY. 'Tis no counterfeit.

SUFFOLK. 'Tis the right ring, by heaven! I told ye all,
    When we first put this dangerous stone a-rolling,
    'Twould fall upon ourselves.

NORFOLK. Do you think, my lords,
    The King will suffer but the little finger
    Of this man to be vex'd?

CHAMBERLAIN. 'Tis now too certain.
    How much more is his life in value with him?
    Would I were fairly out on't!

CROMWELL. My mind gave me,
    In seeking tales and informations
    Against this man, whose honesty the devil
    And his disciples only envy at,
    Ye blew the fire that burns ye. Now have at ye!

[Enter the KING, frowning on them; takes his seat.]

GARDINER. Dread sovereign, how much are we bound to Heaven
    In daily thanks, that gave us such a prince;
    Not only good and wise, but most religious;
    One that, in all obedience, makes the Church
    The chief aim of his honour; and, to strengthen
    That holy duty, out of dear respect,
    His royal self in judgement comes to hear
    The cause betwixt her and this great offender.

KING. You were ever good at sudden commendations,
    Bishop of Winchester. But know, I come not
    To hear such flattery now, and in my presence;
    They are too thin and bare to hide offences.
    To me you cannot reach you play the spaniel,

And think with wagging of your tongue to win me;
But, whatsoe'er thou tak'st me for, I'm sure
Thou hast a cruel nature and a bloody.
[*To Cranmer.*] Good man, sit down. Now let me see the proudest
He, that dares most, but wag his finger at thee:
By all that's holy, he had better starve
Than but once think this place becomes thee not.

SURREY. May it please your Grace,—

KING. No, sir, it does not please me.
I had thought I had had men of some understanding
And wisdom of my council; but I find none.
Was it discretion, lords, to let this man,
This good man,—few of you deserve that title,—
This honest man, wait like a lousy footboy
At chamber-door? and one as great as you are?
Why, what a shame was this! Did my commission
Bid ye so far forget yourselves? I gave ye
Power as he was a councillor to try him,
Not as a groom. There's some of ye, I see,
More out of malice than integrity,
Would try him to the utmost, had ye mean;
Which ye shall never have while I live.

CHANCELLOR. Thus far,
My most dread sovereign, may it like your Grace
To let my tongue excuse all. What was purpos'd
Concerning his imprisonment was rather,
If there be faith in men, meant for his trial
And fair purgation to the world, than malice,
I'm sure, in me.

KING. Well, well, my lords, respect him;
Take him, and use him well, he's worthy of it.
I will say thus much for him, if a prince
May be beholding to a subject, I
Am, for his love and service, so to him.
Make me no more ado, but all embrace him.
Be friends, for shame, my lords! My Lord of Canterbury,
I have a suit which you must not deny me;
That is, a fair young maid that yet wants baptism,
You must be godfather, and answer for her.

CRANMER. The greatest monarch now alive may glory
In such an honour; how may I deserve it,
That am a poor and humble subject to you?

KING. Come, come, my lord, you'd spare your spoons. You shall have
    Two noble partners with you, the old Duchess of Norfolk
    And Lady Marquis Dorset. Will these please you?
    Once more, my Lord of Winchester, I charge you,
    Embrace and love this man.

GARDINER. With a true heart
    And brother-love I do it.

CRANMER. And let Heaven
    Witness how dear I hold this confirmation.

KING. Good man, those joyful tears show thy true heart.
    The common voice, I see, is verified
    Of thee, which says thus, "Do my Lord of Canterbury
    A shrewd turn, and he is your friend for ever."
    Come, lords, we trifle time away; I long
    To have this young one made a Christian.
    As I have made ye one, lords, one remain;
    So I grow stronger, you more honour gain.

[*Exeunt.*]

SCENE IV. *The palace yard.*

[*Noise and tumult within. Enter Porter and his Man.*]

PORTER. You'll leave your noise anon, ye rascals; do you take the court for Paris-
    garden? Ye rude slaves, leave your gaping.

VOICE. [*Within*] Good master porter, I belong to the larder.

PORTER. Belong to the gallows, and be hang'd, ye rogue! Is this a place to roar in? Fetch
    me a dozen crab-tree staves, and strong ones; these are but switches to 'em. I'll
    scratch your heads. You must be seeing christenings? Do you look for ale and cakes
    here, you rude rascals?

MAN. Pray, sir, be patient. 'Tis as much impossible,
    Unless we sweep 'em from the door with cannons,
    To scatter 'em, as 'tis to make 'em sleep
    On May-day morning; which will never be.
    We may as well push against Paul's, as stir 'em.

PORTER. How got they in, and be hang'd?

MAN. Alas, I know not: how gets the tide in?
    As much as one sound cudgel of four foot—
    You see the poor remainder—could distribute,
    I made no spare, sir.

PORTER. You did nothing, sir.

MAN. I am not Samson, nor Sir Guy, nor Colbrand,
    To mow 'em down before me; but if I spar'd any
    That had a head to hit, either young or old,
    He or she, cuckold or cuckold-maker,
    Let me ne'er hope to see a chine again;
    And that I would not for a cow, God save her!

VOICE. [*Within*] Do you hear, master porter?

PORTER. I shall be with you presently, good master puppy.—
    Keep the door close, sirrah.

MAN. What would you have me do?

PORTER. What should you do, but knock 'em down by the dozens? Is this Moorfields to muster in? Or have we some strange Indian with the great tool come to court, the women so besiege us? Bless me, what a fry of fornication is at door! On my Christian conscience, this one christening will beget a thousand; here will be father, godfather, and all together.

MAN. The spoons will be the bigger, sir. There is a fellow somewhat near the door, he should be a brazier by his face, for, o' my conscience, twenty of the dog-days now reign in's nose; all that stand about him are under the line, they need no other penance: that fire-drake did I hit three times on the head, and three times was his nose discharged against me; he stands there, like a mortar-piece, to blow us. There was a haberdasher's wife of small wit near him, that rail'd upon me till her pink'd porringer fell off her head, for kindling such a combustion in the state. I miss'd the meteor once, and hit that woman; who cried out "Clubs!" when I might see from far some forty truncheoners draw to her succour, which were the hope o' the Strand, where she was quartered. They fell on; I made good my place; at length they came to the broomstaff to me; I defied 'em still; when suddenly a file of boys behind 'em, loose shot, deliver'd such a shower of pebbles, that I was fain to draw mine honour in, and let 'em win the work. The devil was amongst 'em, I think, surely.

PORTER. These are the youths that thunder at a playhouse, and fight for bitten apples; that no audience but the tribulation of Tower-hill or the limbs of Limehouse, their dear brothers, are able to endure. I have some of 'em in Limbo Patrum, and there they are like to dance these three days; besides the running banquet of two beadles that is to come.

[Enter Lord Chamberlain.]

CHAMBERLAIN. Mercy o' me, what a multitude are here!
    They grow still too; from all parts they are coming
    As if we kept a fair here! Where are these porters,
    These lazy knaves? Ye have made a fine hand, fellows.
    There's a trim rabble let in. Are all these
    Your faithful friends o' the suburbs? We shall have
    Great store of room, no doubt, left for the ladies,
    When they pass back from the christening.

PORTER. An't please your honour,
    We are but men; and what so many may do,
    Not being torn a-pieces, we have done.
    An army cannot rule 'em.

CHAMBERLAIN. As I live,
    If the King blame me for't, I'll lay ye all
    By the heels, and suddenly; and on your heads
    Clap round fines for neglect. Y'are lazy knaves;
    And here ye lie baiting of bombards, when
    Ye should do service. Hark! the trumpets sound;
    They're come already from the christening.
    Go, break among the press, and find a way out
    To let the troops pass fairly; or I'll find
    A Marshalsea shall hold ye play these two months.

PORTER. Make way there for the princess.

MAN. You great fellow,
    Stand close up, or I'll make your head ache.

PORTER. You i' the camlet, get up o' the rail;
    I'll peck you o'er the pales else.

[Exeunt.]

SCENE V. *The palace.*

[*Enter trumpets, sounding; then two Aldermen, Lord Mayor, Garter, CRANMER, DUKE OF NORFOLK with his marshal's staff, DUKE OF SUFFOLK, two Noblemen bearing great standing-bowls for the christening-gifts; then four Noblemen bearing a canopy, under which the DUCHESS OF NORFOLK, godmother, bearing the Child richly habited in a mantle, etc., train borne by a Lady; then follows the MARCHIONESS DORSET, the other godmother, and Ladies. The troop pass once about the stage, and Garter speaks.*]

GARTER. Heaven, from thy endless goodness, send prosperous life, long and ever happy, to the high and mighty Princess of England, Elizabeth!

[*Flourish. Enter KING and GUARD.*]

CRANMER. [*Kneeling*] And to your royal Grace, and the good queen,
My noble partners, and myself, thus pray:
All comfort, joy, in this most gracious lady,
Heaven ever laid up to make parents happy,
May hourly fall upon ye!

KING. Thank you, good Lord Archbishop.
What is her name?

CRANMER. Elizabeth.

KING. Stand up, lord.

[*The King kisses the child.*]

With this kiss take my blessing: God protect thee!
Into whose hand I give thy life.

CRANMER. Amen.

KING. My noble gossips, ye have been too prodigal.
I thank ye heartily; so shall this lady,
When she has so much English.

CRANMER. Let me speak, sir,
For Heaven now bids me; and the words I utter
Let none think flattery, for they'll find 'em truth.
This royal infant—Heaven still move about her!—
Though in her cradle, yet now promises
Upon this land a thousand thousand blessings,
Which time shall bring to ripeness. She shall be—

But few now living can behold that goodness—
A pattern to all princes living with her,
And all that shall succeed. Saba was never
More covetous of wisdom and fair virtue
Than this pure soul shall be. All princely graces,
That mould up such a mighty piece as this is,
With all the virtues that attend the good,
Shall still be doubled on her. Truth shall nurse her,
Holy and heavenly thoughts still counsel her.
She shall be lov'd and fear'd: her own shall bless her;
Her foes shake like a field of beaten corn,
And hang their heads with sorrow. Good grows with her.
In her days every man shall eat in safety,
Under his own vine, what he plants, and sing
The merry songs of peace to all his neighbours.
God shall be truly known; and those about her
From her shall read the perfect ways of honour,
And by those claim their greatness, not by blood.
Nor shall this peace sleep with her; but as when
The bird of wonder dies, the maiden phoenix,
Her ashes new create another heir
As great in admiration as herself;
So shall she leave her blessedness to one,
When heaven shall call her from this cloud of darkness,
Who from the sacred ashes of her honour
Shall star-like rise as great in fame as she was,
And so stand fix'd. Peace, plenty, love, truth, terror,
That were the servants to this chosen infant,
Shall then be his, and like a vine grow to him.
Wherever the bright sun of heaven shall shine,
His honour and the greatness of his name
Shall be, and make new nations. He shall flourish,
And, like a mountain cedar, reach his branches
To all the plains about him. Our children's children
Shall see this, and bless Heaven.

KING. Thou speakest wonders.

CRANMER. She shall be, to the happiness of England,
    An aged princess; many days shall see her,
    And yet no day without a deed to crown it.
    Would I had known no more! but she must die,
    She must, the saints must have her; yet a virgin,
    A most unspotted lily shall she pass
    To the ground, and all the world shall mourn her.

KING. O Lord Archbishop,
  Thou hast made me now a man! Never, before
This happy child, did I get anything.
This oracle of comfort has so pleas'd me,
That when I am in heaven I shall desire
To see what this child does, and praise my Maker.
I thank ye all. To you, my good Lord Mayor,
And you, good brethren, I am much beholding;
I have receiv'd much honour by your presence,
And ye shall find me thankful. Lead the way, lords.
Ye must all see the Queen, and she must thank ye,
She will be sick else. This day, no man think
Has business at his house; for all shall stay.
This little one shall make it holiday.

[*Exeunt.*]

EPILOGUE

'Tis ten to one this play can never please
All that are here. Some come to take their ease,
And sleep an act or two; but those, we fear,
We have frighted with our trumpets; so, 'tis clear,
They'll say 'tis nought: others, to hear the city
Abus'd extremely, and to cry "That's witty!"
Which we have not done neither: that, I fear,
All the expected good we're like to hear
For this play at this time, is only in
The merciful construction of good women;
For such a one we show'd 'em. If they smile
And say 'twill do, I know, within a while
All the best men are ours; for 'tis ill hap
If they hold when their ladies bid 'em clap.

THE END

Breinigsville, PA USA
30 June 2010

240885BV00003B/168/P